NORSE MYTHOLOGY

The Vikings and their Lore
from Gods and Goddesses
to Midgard and Valhalla

DAGMAR NYLUND

CONTENTS

Introduction

Norse mythology is a vibrant and distinctive lore that is vast and intriguing. As with many other popular mythologies, its influences are still seen around the world today. Movies, books, and even music involving these mythologies bring awareness back to these fascinating ancient civilizations. Without meaning to, we are learning more and more about Norse mythology.

But how much of it is true? Is what we see in the media a reflection of how things truly were for Vikings of old, or has everything gone through a sensationalist filter for the benefit of a contemporary audience? How can we distinguish between historic facts and modern creations driven by plot?

This book aims to bring to light the lifestyle and culture of the Vikings, their lore and their everyday lives. The following chapters will uncover myriad aspects of the Viking world, including their art, architecture, clothing and even makeup. Famed Viking leaders will also be introduced, legends in their own right.

We will take an in-depth look at the mythical creatures and beings that spring straight from the poems of old. There will be discussions surrounding all aspects of the divine, from gods and goddesses to the nine realms of the World Tree and the lore involving them.

There is much to get through, but before we jump into Norse mythology, let us first learn about what mythology is and how it can help us understand a people.

CHAPTER 1

Mythic Beginnings

Norse mythology is an exciting and complex set of lore linked closely with the Vikings. To better understand this world, we will first look briefly at what mythology itself signifies and entails.

Mythology

Mythology—from the Greek *mythos* for "story of the people" and *logos* for "word" or "speech"—refers to the collection of information pertaining to the understanding of a people. In other words, mythology is the set of stories that reflect the beliefs of a social group, such as the Vikings. These cultural stories could be about the origins of humanity, the distinction between good and evil, the existence of deities and mystical creatures, life and death, traditions, superstitions and human nature.

Myths, legends and folklore all fall into the category of mythology. This book aims to shed light on the mythology of the Vikings as well as their history, religion, beliefs, practices and way of life.

Types of Mythology

There are different types of myths, namely:

- etiological myths

- historical myths

- psychological myths

Etiological myths deal with the origin of things. They explain why something is the way it is or how it came to be.

Historical myths explain events from the past with heightened lessons and meanings.

Psychological myths link the mental and physical aspects of understanding the human psyche. Often seen in journeys of self-discovery or understanding, these myths sometimes overlap with folktales.

The Difference Between Myths, Legends and Folklore

Myths, legends and folklore are often used interchangeably; however, subtle differences exist between them that highlight the margins between reality and fiction. What many believe to be history may actually be myth, and vice versa.

Because these tales have been passed down through word of mouth in the form of poems, songs and stories, their legitimacy can be questioned. However, by truly delving into the sources and appreciating the mix of creativity, evolution of stories over time and historical basis, we can begin to see folklore's broader picture.

The below terms, while similar, hold distinct meanings when it comes to evaluating the history of a people. All, however, are necessary in order to create a more complete view of life in the Viking era.

myth, noun

A symbolic narrative, usually of unknown origin and at least partly traditional, that ostensibly relates actual events and that is especially associated with religious belief. Myths are specific accounts of gods or superhuman beings involved in extraordinary events or circumstances in a time that is unspecified but which is understood as existing apart from ordinary human experience.

In simple terms, myths may refer to stories about human origins and religious or divine beings. The beings could be deities, ethereal creatures or demigods. Myths are known to be sacred and are usually passed down by priests and scholars to teach moral lessons or to account for the theories behind known events. Essentially, myths are stories that explain the universe, the world and nature, albeit in a poetic manner.

It is arguable that myths are fiction owing to the divine and fantastical nature of their storytelling

One famous myth is that of the Greek goddess Persephone. Persephone is the daughter of Demeter, the goddess of grain and harvests, who was kidnapped by Hades, the god of the underworld. Hades fell in love with Persephone when he spied her playing in the flower fields. He concocted a plan with Zeus, his brother, to kidnap the girl while her mother was distracted and make her his wife.

And so Persephone was taken to the underworld. While they were enemies at first, Persephone grew to love Hades in time. Demeter, however, never stopped looking for her daughter. After a time, she begged Zeus to bring her daughter back.

Through negotiations, it was determined that Persephone would spend four months in the underworld with her husband, Hades, and eight months above ground with her mother, Demeter. She would then return to the underworld and repeat the cycle for the rest of eternity.

This is the story behind the seasons in ancient Greece. Winter months were seen as the time when Demeter was most saddened, when her daughter resided in the underworld. Spring and summer reflected the times when the goddess of nature happily had her daughter back. And so the cycle of Persephone, the cycle of the seasons, began.

Other examples of myths include the stories of:

- Adam and Eve
- Hercules
- Odin
- Icarus
- Anubis
- Krishna

legend, noun

A traditional story or group of stories told about a particular person or place. They may include supernatural beings, elements of mythology or explanations of natural phenomena, but they are associated with a specific locality or person and are told as a matter of history.

Legends are stories based on historical events or people whose origins may be unverifiable, due in part to the oral nature of many narratives. Legends are often exaggerated and contain lofty ideals. Unlike myths, they are not meant to teach morals or beliefs, but rather to influence cultural actions.

Legends can be passed down both orally and through literature, disseminated by scholars and commoners alike. They may also deal with otherworldly creatures and beings in a manner similar to myths. As such, there is an overlap between the classifications of myth and legend.

Many know the legend of King Arthur and his Knights of the Round Table. But how much of that tale is based in truth, and how much has succumbed to hyperbole and fantasy?

Other examples of legends include those of:

- Genghis Khan
- Atlantis
- Tages
- Mulan
- Beowulf
- King Arthur
- William Tell

folklore, noun

The sum total of traditionally derived oral literature, material culture (such as tools, art and clothing) and custom of subcultures within mostly literate and technologically advanced societies. Folklore often refers solely to the oral literature tradition.

Folklore comprises secular stories—folktales— created for entertainment. Unlike legends and myths, these tales are considered purely fictional and are usually spread orally by common people.

Because myths and legends are based on historical events, an assumed time and place is associated with them. Folklore differs in that the time and place are not usually essential to the larger narrative, which exists to entertain and, in some cases, teach lessons.

Most superstitions are rooted in folklore, which is the reason for disparity in traditional cultural practices across regions.

An example of a folktale is the story "The Boy Who Cried Wolf." A mischievous shepherd boy watching the village flock plays pranks on his fellow villagers, yelling "Wolf!" in terror and laughing at those who come running to his aid. Until the day he encounters a real black wolf approaching from the woods. The villagers hear his cries of "Wolf!" as another prank and do not go to the boy. The boy watches in regret as the sheep are eaten by the wolf.

This story, while sad, has prevailed through the years with the value of being both entertaining and forewarning. It is told to the youth of a community to deter them from lying or deceiving.

Many versions of this tale exist, albeit in different contexts, in various communities across the world and through the ages. While the story offers no insight into the origins of a people, it clarifies how a society operates, what its moral compasses are and what the community values. Just because the tale isn't based in reality does not lessen its value as a tool for understanding people and offering guidance.

Other examples of folktales are:

- "The Three Little Pigs"
- "Hansel and Gretel"
- "Aladdin"
- "Cinderella"

Famous Mythologies

There is a vast number of distinct mythologies found worldwide. Every society and region may provide a wholly separate mythology that can provide understanding in the nature and ideal of humankind.

Greek

Greek mythology is one of the most well-known in the world. Recurring often in pop culture, it is one of the most accessible ancient lores available today. Many may be familiar with the story of Zeus becoming the leader of the gods after defeating his father, Kronos.

The myth chronicles how Kronos feared his children, as it was foretold they would overthrow him in the same way he had overthrown his own father. In a stream of paranoia, Kronos ate each of the children born to his wife, Rhea, shortly after their births.

Rhea grew tired of seeing her children devoured, so she tricked Kronos into swallowing a rock wrapped in swaddling clothes and instead hid Zeus on Crete to be raised in secret.

When Zeus was grown, he returned to face his father. He tricked Kronos into drinking something that made him vomit up Zeus' brothers and sisters that he had previously swallowed. They then all banded together to slay their father, bringing an end to the era of the Titans, the older gods and goddesses in Greek mythology, and giving rise to the Olympians.

The tale of Zeus and Kronos is an example of an etiological myth, an origin story that explains why something is the way it is—in this case, how the Olympians rose to power in Greek mythology.

Egyptian

Egyptian lore is as deep and vast as Egypt's deserts. There is no shortage of stories in Egyptian mythology.

The story of Isis and Osiris is an excellent example of how a myth can be psychological, as it depicts the reasoning behind human tradition and ritual.

The story follows Osiris, who married Isis after becoming the ruler of Egypt. Osiris was well-liked by the people. His brother Set, becoming jealous, tricked and killed Osiris, leaving his devastated wife behind. Set scattered his brother's remains across the lands to hide them from Isis.

Isis, unable to bear the loss, went in search of his body. She used magic to put the pieces of his body back together and embalm it with oils. This is described as the first practice of embalming. Osiris came back to life and, with Isis, conceived a child, Horus, the hawk god. Osiris was then free to descend to the afterlife, where he became king of the underworld.

This tale illustrates how the practice of preserving bodies after death arose from the belief that the souls of the departed may one day return. Embalming thus came to be common in funeral rituals across the country.

Indian

Indian mythology contains another rich well of stories that are increasing in popularity around the world. One of these folktales is entitled "Between Two Wives."

The story tells of a man with two wives, one much younger than him and one near his age. The wives would argue frequently and so he built them each a home in different parts of town to limit contact between them. An arrangement was reached in which he agreed to split his days equally between the two wives.

He experienced a different life in each home. Whenever he stayed with the younger wife, she would try to make him look more youthful by plucking out his gray hairs. When he stayed with the older wife, she would pluck out his dark hairs as she did not want him looking younger than her.

In the end, the man was left bald without a single hair on his head.

Folktales are clearly meant to entertain and, in some cases, educate. Perhaps the lesson here is you can only please others so far.

Japanese

Japanese mythology boasts a unique blend of expression that draws influence from Japan's two main religions, Buddhism and Shinto, as well as agriculture-based folk religion. A number of Japanese myths involve famed creatures known as kitsune, or mythical foxes. These creatures are known to be highly intelligent, with the ability to shapeshift at will. Lore states that the kitsune will grow a tail for every 100 years it has lived on earth; thus, many-tailed foxes are a common motif in Japanese culture.

The most powerful kitsune are the nine-tailed foxes. They are prophesied to have infinite knowledge and power.

Two types of foxes, known as Zenko and Yako, illustrate some of the distinct personality quirks of Japanese mythical creatures. Zenko are kind souls with magical powers, said to be the messengers of the god Inari. A number of shrines are dedicated to them around Japan, and they continue to be important cultural symbols. They represent good harvest, fertility and prosperity. The Yako are known as mischievous fox spirits who love to play pranks on humans or cause trouble wherever they go.

The Japanese kitsune are examples of creatures relevant and important to a set of mythology.

The History of Norse Mythology

Norse mythology refers to the set of myths upheld by Northern Europeans in and around modern-day Scandinavia around the period of 790-1100 AD, known as the Viking Age. Scandinavia includes the countries of Denmark, Norway and Sweden, although the Norse people living there in this time managed to travel extensively, exploring, raiding and relocating as they went. Norse mythology is known as a preserved form of older Germanic Paganism and also resembles basic Anglo-Saxon mythology.

As with many cultures, Norse mythology was passed down orally through prose—poetry, to be exact—for many years until it was finally transcribed in the 13th century AD, when the Edda texts were first written.

The Poetic Edda—sometimes called the Elder Edda—contains descriptions and renderings of pre-Christian Germanic deities, heroes, and themes. While written in c. 1270, the Edda draws on content from previous centuries, from the Viking age of Norse mythology. As some of the only known written sources of Norse myths, the Eddas are critical in the development of the Nordic cosmos.

Skaldic poetry also adds to our view of Norse mythology from Scandinavian folklore. Skalds were old Norse poets, and the style they developed was a bit more precise in measure and fanciful in word choice than the Edda content. Skaldic poetry was generally associated with specific, named poets, whereas the Poetic Edda was anonymous.

Most texts that form the fundamentals of Norse mythology were written in Iceland, where direct descendants of Vikings still maintained interest in the way of life. It was around the 13th century AD that an Icelandic poet and chieftain named Snorri Sturluson collated all available works on Norse mythology and wrote the Prose Edda—called the Younger Edda. The Prose Edda interpreted Norse mythology for audiences of the time.

The Prose Edda comprises four sections: the prologue, Gylfaginning, Skáldskaparmál, and Háttatal. The Prologue is a summary of the Norse gods, introducing them and their characteristics. The Gylfaginning is a collection of questions and answers pertaining to specific aspects of Norse mythology. The Skáldskaparmál is a guide to figures of speech and the like. The Háttatal is a composition of Skaldic poetry.

The Norse sagas provide another perspective of the Viking worldview and history. Falling somewhere in the mix of fantastical legend and reality, these many stories, told in a straightforward manner, depict adventures of heroes, kings and families. First written down in 13th-century Iceland, these originally oral histories of previous generations contain elements of both mythology and history. While their accuracy may be hard to measure, they offer a fascinating look at historical Viking storytelling.

As the above texts were among the first surviving written works on Vikings and their mythology, they form the backbone of everything we understand about Vikings today. It is from these sources that we gain our understanding of the Norse cosmos and everything it contains.

Norse Cosmos

The term cosmos refers to the universe as well as one's perspective on how the universe is organized, based on cultural beliefs and background. The Norse have a fairly well-ordered and somewhat fascinating view of how the universe came to be and the structure it took.

In the Beginning

According to the texts, it is said that before anything existed, there was a vast, empty blackness called Ginnungagap. Through the ever-changing nature of chaos, this void spurred the creation of the realms of Niflheim and Muspelheim.

Niflheim lay to the north and was a land of ice, frost and snow. It was said to be a cold and dark place where nothing could grow or flourish.

In the south, Muspelheim was a land of raging fire and lava, where the very soot in the air caught alight and burned. This would become the home of the great fire giant, Surtr, and other fire-bearing creatures.

Giants

In the gap where Niflheim and Muspelheim met, lava melted ice and a humanoid shape emerged from the drops. Ymir, the first of the giants, came to be. Fed on the teats of the great cow Audhumbla, who also manifested in the seam between worlds, Ymir was the first of the Jötnar (pronounced YOT-nar).

The Jötnar (often translated as "giants," although not necessarily giant in stature) were symbols of chaotic elementalism. These powerful beings could represent the unrealized potential of chaotic energy.

Thus, Ymir was a hermaphrodite who could reproduce asexually. After falling asleep, Ymir grew two more giant offspring—one male and one female—from the sweat under his arms. His legs joined to create a third, Thrudgelmir, or "Strength Yeller." This became the first family of Jötnar to exist.

Gods

The great cow Audhumbla, from which Ymir had fed, nourished herself on a block of salty ice, repeatedly licking it for sustenance. The ice slowly uncovered Buri, the first of the Æsir gods to come into existence. The Æsir are the main family of Norse gods. Buri bore a son called Bor who, with his wife Bestla, sired the first half-god, half-giant children: Odin, Vili, and Ve.

Fearful of the giants outnumbering the Æsir, Odin and his twin brothers decided to ambush and kill Ymir one night while he slept. The resulting battle caused such a wave of blood that most of the giants drowned in it. Only Bergelmir and his wife survived the battle and escaped to find a safe place in the land of mist. It is said that all future giants are heirs of these two.

Earth

The earth was created out of Ymir's corpse by Odin, Vili, and Ve. They dragged his body to the center of Ginnungagap. Translated directly from the Poetic Edda ("The Song of Grimner," 1861), the story of how Ymir was transformed into the earth reads:

From Ymer's flesh, in the dawning of time, was made

The earth, and from his blood the raging sea,

The rocks from his bones, and from his hair

the trees,

And plants; his skull became the vaulted heaven;

And Midgard, from his fringed lids, the gods

Kindly have fashioned for the sons of men;

And from his brain, the clouds that dress the sky

Of Summer, or dart their lightnings in the storm,

Their first substance had.

Dwarves

Dwarves were formed from the worms that escaped Ymir's rotting remains while Odin and his brothers were creating the earth.

Afraid that the sky they had created would fall, they sent one dwarf to each of the four corners of the world to hold up the sky. They were named Nordi, Austri, Sundri, and Vestri, corresponding to the four cardinal directions, north, east, south and west.

The rest of the dwarves made their dwellings in the rock underground, which came to be known as Svartalfheim, the home of the dwarves. Dwarves became expert miners and craftspeople, specializing in creating beautiful jewelry and powerful weapons.

Sun and Moon

Sol and Mani are the sun and moon of the Norse cosmos. They sprung into existence when the cosmos was being created but did not know what their powers were or what to do with themselves. As such, they wandered freely until the gods ordered them to follow a schedule to light up the sky.

Humans

One day when walking on the beach, the Æsir discovered two tree trunks, one ash and one elm. They each bestowed gifts upon the trunks, breathing life into them. Odin blessed the logs with spirit and life. Ve gave them movement, mind, and intelligence. Vili gave them shape, speech, feelings, and their five senses.

And so the first man and woman came to be. Named Ask and Embla, respectively, these two humans were placed in the safety of a world called Midgard, fashioned from the eyelashes of Ymir and protected on all sides by a huge wall.

Ask and Embla behaved much the same as the Gods—they ate, hunted, fished, married and reproduced. Humankind flourished and the population grew. Societies were erected, politics developed and art manifested.

So where did the Vikings come from? And what made them Vikings to begin with?

The next chapter will introduce the history of Vikings, how they came to be and where they came from.

CHAPTER 2
Viking Beginnings

Vikings—sometimes called Norsemen—were a seafaring group of people who migrated through Northern Europe during the period of c. 800 to 1100 AD, which came to be known as the Viking Age. No one can attest to why the Vikings began moving, though many speculate it was because of harsh winters and food scarcity.

The start of the Viking Age can be marked by the raid on the monastery of Lindisfarne, an island off the northeast coast of modern-day England, in 793. Thus began the first of the migrations of the Vikings from Scandinavia. This event of burning, plundering and raiding a religious institute would set the tone for how Vikings would then be perceived for much of the Viking Age.

Why Are They Called Vikings?

The word "Viking" stems from the Old Norse Scandinavian word *víkingr,* meaning "pirate." Vikings became known for being pirates, raiders, settlers and traders and were feared for their strength, savagery and ruthlessness.

The term Viking did not refer to a race of people but more toward the behavior of raiding parties. It was a term directed toward any pirating group seen as uncivilized and un-Christian.

It is also debated as to whether Norse women and children were referred to as Vikings, as the original word applied to raiders and settlers, who were predominantly men. In the same way, men who were not warriors, such as farmers, blacksmiths and others with non-fighting jobs, may also not have been referred to as Vikings.

In modern times, however, it is accepted by historians to refer to the entire community of Norse settlers—men, women, and children—as Vikings for the sake of simplicity and clarity. For the purposes of this book, 'Viking' shall refer to all Norse folk alive during the Viking Age.

Where Did Vikings Live?

The Vikings, also known as Norsemen since the early 19th century, lived in the northern European region of Scandinavia. Much of their homeland was rural, with many people making their earnings off agriculture or fishing.

A mass migration of the Norse people began with the Lindisfarne raid in 793. No one knows what caused the Vikings to become restless and begin moving. Some speculate that food shortages were a growing concern among an ever-increasing population. Others think the temptation of new wealth in neighboring countries became too difficult to turn from. There are even a few who believe it was an attempt at world domination and power acquisition. Regardless of the reason, the migration occurred, and Vikings began creating new settlements across most of Northern Europe, Western Russia and even North America.

Some of the first regions they settled were the Scottish Isles and much of the Baltic Sea. Other nearby regions like the Carolingian Empire and modern-day England and Ireland suffered through many decades of attacks and plundering before Vikings decided on permanent settlements within these areas.

In these instances, land was either seized by force or by agreements made with the previous landowners.

It was this conquering mindset and determination that led to the Vikings expanding their raids across the world. Finding new, uninhabited lands became something of an achievement among the Vikings. Their advance spread east and south to Russia, Constantinople (the capital of the Byzantine Empire, known today as Istanbul, Turkey), the Middle East and North Africa. Their western expansion pressed on to the Faroe Islands, Iceland, Greenland and even North America, five centuries before Christopher Columbus.

The Vikings were thought to have created settlements on the Faroe Islands in the early 9th century to erect a trading post and stopping point between Norway and Iceland, their new venture at the time.

Iceland was discovered by Vikings around the mid-9th century, with Ingólf Arnarson and his raiders settling there in 872. They established themselves as an independent society, severing all allegiance with Norway and subsequently creating their own governing body. Chiefs would gather on a regular basis to discuss everything from trade to population growth and social welfare. As such, Iceland is said to have the oldest parliament in recorded history.

Vikings were not only raiders but skilled tradespeople as well. A lucrative trade market was instituted at every settlement and port they came into contact with. New trade routes developed quickly between these regions as new developments were made in the shipbuilding industry. These ships allowed for large loads and faster travel as compared with those of most other shipping companies in operation at the time.

Trade networks were founded from as far east as Russia's Volga River and Constantinople and west to Dublin, Ireland and Newfoundland, Canada. As expeditions increased, these trade networks expanded north to Greenland, east to Kyiv, and as far south as the Mediterranean Sea.

By the mid-11th century, the raids slowly began to subside. Final expeditions were royally sponsored in order to fully conquer any remaining lands. The emperor Cnut the Great was one such sponsor, reigning over Denmark, Norway and England.

At this point, Vikings had complete control over large parts of Scotland and other areas near Dublin. Normandy was under the full reign of Rollo, a Viking who had been granted the land in 911 by King Charles of West Francia.

Much of western Russia and almost all of Ukraine had seen settlements of Swedish Vikings since the mid-9th century. Permanent bases were established around Novgorod and Kyiv.

What Did Vikings Do?

Prior to the raids that began in 793, Norse folk were farmers and fishermen, living a life of rural work and pleasures. They relied on well-tilled soil and well-supplied fishing grounds to survive, as well as gathered materials.

Because of the remote nature of their homelands, they also had to be self-sufficient in creating tools and weapons. They became particularly proficient at metalsmithing. This won them the envy of the numerous other regions they traded with and would lead to a lucrative trade market in the future.

While much changed during their period of migration and expansion, Vikings pretty much lived and behaved the same way they had previously, albeit with a growing number of warriors in their company.

Some individuals did change roles. Others took on additional mantles. Relatively peaceful fishermen could become brutal seafaring warriors, pillaging coastal cities and towns for supplies and treasure. Norsemen became known as Vikings only when they attacked and settled across the shores of Northern Europe.

In addition to the increase in warriors and seafarers, another industry that saw growth was the trade market. Suddenly traders, artisans, and boat masters had access to a whole new world of trade. The production of high-quality goods, like jewelry and tools, skyrocketed.

An abundance of new jobs became available in every area the Vikings settled. Each base required much of the same things, for example, a smithy, a healer, a tradesperson or a weaver. There was no shortage of tasks, with many Vikings juggling several positions at once.

What Did Vikings Look Like?

When people think about Vikings, they may be likely to picture massive long-haired warriors with large muscles, covered in battle scars, beards (the males, at least) and grime. Shows like Netflix's *Vikings*, Marvel's *Thor* movies or video games like *Assassin's Creed: Valhalla* may be responsible for how Vikings are depicted and understood by modern society.

While some of these descriptions are accurate, some traits may be a little off-track. Let's explore how Vikings really looked during the Viking Age.

Build

The average Viking male stood around 5'7" (171 cm) tall, with Viking females closer to 5'2" (158 cm). This may seem small by our modern standards, with a current average Scandinavian height of roughly 5'11" (180 cm) for men and 5'5" (166 cm) for women. However, Vikings were actually among the tallest people in the Middle Ages, towering over other nationalities by several inches.

Both the men and women were of a heftier build, with prominent muscles and large fat storage. This can be attributed to their habitat and lifestyles. Manual labor such as fishing, farming and home construction naturally yielded larger muscles. Warriors involved in ongoing raids through the years were even more renowned for their strength, giving them a larger-than-life appearance.

Size was a major theme and identifier in old epics. Many Vikings were named after their massive size, as physical power was revered among warriors. Gǫngu-Hrólfr, known as the "Walking Rollo," was described as being too big to ride a horse. Björn Ironside was said to be so physically powerful that he could not be harmed in battle. Thorkell the Tall was the leader of the Jomsvikings mercenary order and named one of the tallest warriors in Viking history. St. Olaf the Stout was so sturdy and dense that he survived being shot out of a cannon—several times!

The poems of old reveal great feats of strength among Vikings, though much of this has been labeled as speculation or hyperbole owing to the romanticized nature of these tales. Archeological excavations, however, have unearthed heavily-muscled Viking bodies that would have weighed around 300 lbs (135 kg) at the time they were alive. It is hard to say whether these findings were the norm for the time or if they were more indicative of a specifically warrior physique. While the Viking Museum of Oslo displays some beefy examples of Nordic individuals, they may have been more built as a result of their warrior training and lifestyles.

What Made Vikings So Strong?

Vikings were a warrior clan who trained their young to fight as soon as they could walk. Everyone learned combat skills—even farmers and fishermen. This became especially true once the raids began. With this new expansion, it became clear that everyone needed to learn to fight, whether to protect one's own land or to pillage others' land. This training, combined with a steady diet of bread, fish and pork, produced a nation of stout, heavily-muscled people.

It is worth pointing out that being a Viking was more a lifestyle than an ethnicity. Because of the lifestyle, you had to be incredibly strong or risk falling in battle.

Facial Features

An interesting attribute of the Vikings was the almost androgynous look of their people. The visual facial distinctions between men and women were few and overlapping. Men had what modern people would consider more feminine facial characteristics, such as slimmer, rounder faces with delicate features. Women, on the other hand, had more masculine-type facial features, such as more pronounced foreheads and square jawlines.

For this reason, it can be difficult to identify the gender of skeletons found in Viking regions. Were it not for clothing—and, in the case of most men, beards—many would struggle to tell the difference. Even archaeologists can have a hard time identifying genders from facial features alone. Examination of the pelvic bones is a helpful tool, as female pelvic bones are generally wider to accommodate childbirth.

Also of note, due to the sea-trader life of the Vikings, they had a great amount of interaction with other cultures and peoples around the world. This would often result in offspring. As such, no "pure" Viking bloodlines exist. The closest resemblance to Vikings of old would be modern-day Scandinavians.

Eyes

Similar to Nordic populations of the present, around 50–80% of Vikings (region dependent) would have blue, green, or hazel eyes.

Hair

Through genetic research and the examination of drawings and artwork, it has been determined that the majority of Vikings were red-haired or blond. Different regions had different propensities. West Scandinavia (Denmark), for example, showed a higher number of redheads than North Scandinavia (Stockholm), where blond hair was dominant.

Dark-haired Vikings did exist; however, as it was fashionable at the time to have lighter hair, many dark-haired Vikings would lighten their locks using lye soaps and other substances made out of animal fats and ash. These products also had the benefit of treating head lice and scalp infections, both of which were common problems of the time.

Beards

Almost all depictions of men and gods (with the exception of Loki) are shown to have full beards and mustaches. These range from close-cut goatees to long, flowing beards and even braided sideburns.

Vikings have quite often been depicted as having elaborate and beautifully neat facial hair. Older men often had longer, more intricate beards, while younger men and laborers had more practical facial hair, such as full mustaches with heavy mutton chops. Regardless of the style, almost all men had facial hair.

Facial hair was a mark of pride for a man. Because of the significance of facial hair in Norse society, it is believed that men without the ability to grow proper facial hair—or those that chose not to—were ridiculed by their neighbors. Such mockery is frequently seen in Norse mythology. Lack of adequate facial hair was a means to taunt and insult one another, while at the same time, insulting a man's beard was grounds for him to retaliate with murder, if he wished.

As with size, beards are another identifying feature that many Viking warriors became known for. Svein Tveskägg

(Forkbeard) was known for his beard, which was split into two braids.

Hygiene

Another feature of Vikings is that they were dirty. Right? Perhaps by modern standards; however, for the time, Vikings were seen as cleaner and more hygienic than the Anglo-Saxons of England.

This allowed Viking men to have some success with English women, who thought that they were cleaner and far more pleasant smelling than their native men. Just because they were warriors and lived a semi-nomadic lifestyle did not mean that they were filthy.

English chronicler John Wallingford, around 1220, describes the grooming habits of Viking men as follows (S, Jessica, 2019):

"They [had] also conquered, or planned to conquer, all the country's best cities and caused many hardships for the country's original citizens for they were—according to their country's customs—in the habit of combing their hair every day, to bath every Saturday, to change their clothes frequently and to draw attention to themselves by means of many frivolous whims. It is in this way that they sieged the married women's virtue and persuaded the daughters of even noble men to become their mistresses."

As shown in Wallingford's journals, the Vikings dedicated every Saturday, also called Laugardagr or Lördag, from the Old Norse roots for "pool" and "day," as the day on which they bathed.

Archeologists have found evidence of grooming tools in ancient Viking sites. Items such as tweezers, combs, nail and ear cleaners and toothpicks were all found in the home. Combs were usually kept by both men and women, carried in a pouch on the belt.

As we can see, Vikings are a complex and often misunderstood group with more to offer than many imagine. It may be hard to look past the image of a filthy, savage barbarian who kills anything in its path, even when evidence shows that they were, in fact, a neat and clean bunch who looked after their appearance.

As for their brutality and cruelty, later chapters will explore the validity of these perceptions and uncover further complexities of Viking society and behavior.

CHAPTER 3
Nordic Culture

Yes, Vikings had culture! And art! They had particular ways of clothing and housing themselves and of navigating the abundant waters around their lands. They had an eye for visual appeal and cultural significance as well as function in the objects of their daily lives.

To get a more balanced and detailed picture of Viking life, we look to their various cultural expressions and contributions. Norse clothing, jewelry, armor, makeup and hairstyles give us a more enhanced view of what they looked like. Viking art and architecture, as well as their impressive shipbuilding skills and unique Runic writing system, are also covered.

Clothing

Two things that scientists know about old Norse attire are: Vikings loved wearing colors, and Vikings did not have horns on their helmets.

When people think of Viking clothes, they tend to picture dark colors, thick furs and possibly, horned helmets. While some of that is accurate, our image of the Viking wardrobe has seen some adjustment in recent years.

Evidence from grave sites and other archeological digs has shown that Vikings had a love of bright colors and patterned clothes. Blue and red were among the most popular colors. Patterns, particularly plaid, were also favored.

Most clothing was made from wool or linen, also called flax, the plant from which linen is derived. As a rough, sturdy fabric, wool was often used to make the outer layers of clothes, while linen was softer and used for undergarments.

The National Museum in Denmark states that linen has comprised about 40% of fabric found from the Viking age. Linen is incredibly difficult to weave and, thus, also expensive to buy. It can take about 44 pounds (20 kg) of flax plants to fabricate a single tunic. It is, however, a very durable and long-lasting material, ideal for a rural people like the Vikings. It is thought that poorer Vikings, who could not afford linen undergarments, slept in the nude.

Richer Vikings could afford to wear silk. As silk was imported, only the most privileged or well-traveled Vikings owned the fabric. Semi-wealthy Vikings may have used silk trims on their cloaks or tunics, but only the truly rich could afford whole silk garments. Golden thread and sewn-on ribbons were also in fashion for the affluent of society.

Excavations showed evidence of silver buttons and jewelry being used across both genders. The styles of these more elegant clothes were heavily influenced by the Byzantine courts of the time.

Women

Women usually wore close-fitting dresses over long undergowns. These dresses were called "harness dresses," or *hangrok*, and were held together at the shoulders by two large buckles and a leather strap over each shoulder. Later remnants of clothing found indicated that some of their dresses had built-in gussets, specialized fabric panels for extra support and shape.

Because of the cold and modesty, women wore two layers. Their underlayer was made of a soft linen base. This was used to cool the skin and absorb sweat. The outer clothes were usually made of a sturdier wool, for warmth and durability.

Underclothes could reflect various local fashions as their shape and style could vary by region. Where some women preferred plainer underlayers, others favored pleated versions.

Rectangular cloaks were worn during colder months to protect from cold, wind and, in some cases, light rain. They were secured over the shoulders by a small brooch. The cloak was usually made of a heavy wool and sometimes decorated with bands of fur or intricate embroidery. Fashions also saw the rise of dual-color reversible cloaks.

Woven fabric belts were worn around the waist with satchels and bags for small articles like purses, sewing items, fire starters and small knives.

Women could choose between a hat or a scarf. Older women were more fond of scarves, while hats were favored by outdoor workers. It is thought that the type of head coverings worn may have been a way of distinguishing between married and unmarried women.

Viking women wore the same shoes as men: sewn leather or sheepskin, fastened with a shoelace around the lower ankle. Because hardened soles were not used, shoes tended to wear out frequently. But the abundance of leather in Viking times meant this was not a great problem, even for the poorest of Vikings.

Men

Viking men also wore two layers. Their underlayer consisted of a linen kirtle: a long shirt that fell to their knees. Depending on the weather, they might wear a high-necked plain tunic over this. Showing the chest area was considered feminine, so many men favored high-necked outer layers. In some cases, drawstrings were used to close the neckline.

Men wore pants that could vary in roominess and design, with many reaching just below the knees. In warmer months, they were often shorter, but long pants were rarely worn, despite the cold regions. Studies think this may have been due to mobility restrictions. Instead, leg wrappings were used to keep the leg warm and protected, consisting of long pieces of sturdy fabric wrapped from knee to toe. These protected against injuries caused by forest brush or frostbite.

Cloaks were similar in style to women's. However, they were worn gathered over one arm to allow the wearer to freely wield an ax or sword. This also made it easy to establish at a glance if a Viking was right-handed or left-handed. Some cloaks, particularly those of fishermen or those residing in snowy regions, were slightly waterproofed by rubbing tallow, rendered beef or mutton fat, or wax on the lining.

Men's belts served for holding objects, like those of women, as well as possibly for holding up the pants. These belts could carry items like a small ax, fire starter kit, comb, money, gambling beads, and even nail cleaner. Made of leather, they were held together by ornate buckles. The ends of the belt might hang down the front of the tunic, and the free end was often embellished as well. Typical belt thickness has been estimated to be about ¾ inch. Thicker belts were used to hold up swords and larger axes.

Men often wore caps on their heads. Made of wool, sheepskin or leather, they could be pointed or round. They typically consisted of three triangular pieces of fabric sewn together to fit the head. Wool-lined ear flaps could be added to protect against wind and bitter temperatures. Another hood-like covering called a höttr was used in colder months. Covering the head, neck and shoulders, it left an opening for just the face.

Sometimes, furs of animals were worn by accomplished hunters. Bear or wolf skins could symbolize a superior warrior status.

There were no significant differences between the shoes of women and men. Men's shoes, like women's, were made of leather or sheepskin.

Children

Children wore simplified versions of adult clothing, such as basic tunics and pants for boys and simple overdresses for girls.

Jewelry

Jewelry was worn by both men and women. The most common pieces were brooches, rings and beads. Often made of gold, silver and iron, the detailed and intricate designs of Viking jewelry made it valuable across the world.

In desperate times or when trading, jewelry was often used as bullion, bulk metal sold by weight and used for the making of coins. It was an easy item over which to haggle. In fact, the word "haggle" in the English language is Old Norse in origin, coming from the word *hǫggva* for "hew," meaning to chop or cut.

Jewelry was displayed in a number of ways. Glass or amber beads were strung between brooches for added adornment or worn around the neck in general.

Arm, neck and finger rings were quite popular. Although the Vikings knew about earrings through their travels, they were never popularized within the culture.

Brooches held together dresses and cloaks or were used purely for ornamentation. Women also often used them to fasten purses or other small items to their dresses, as pockets were not part of Viking clothing design.

Jewelry was hence not only a display of beauty but also of wealth. And, as the Vikings believed they would need money in the afterlife as well, the dead were often buried with their jewelry.

Armor

Armor was expensive and labor-intensive to create. Items like mail, commonly called chain mail, required thousands of interlinking pieces to be hand riveted together to form one piece of armor. Most warriors, therefore, did not have full kits of armor but rather just a few seasoned pieces, probably handed down through the family line or won in a battle conquest.

Mail shirts were the most common armor pieces, used as protection from sharp weapons. Long-sleeved and hanging below the knee, they were worn over a padded undershirt to prevent blisters.

Helmet use is difficult to quantify. There is scant physical evidence of helmets found, and most of it is in the form of fragments that are hard to reconstruct or verify. Iron, as with armor in general, was not readily available at the time and was quite expensive. Many Vikings may have gone without headgear. Or, if they had a helmet, it may have been made from leather as much as iron. Metal helmets that were present appear to have been bowl-shaped with a nose guard down the front. Fancier versions may have included ornate flaps that covered the sides of the face, forming a mask around the eyes. And, regardless of type, they did not have horns.

Where Did the Horned-Helmet Myth Come From?
Horned helmets were not used by the Vikings. Or, at least, not in battle. Horns would have easily become tangled in a cloak or grabbed while fighting.

It was perhaps only around the end of the 19th century that Vikings started appearing in the media with horned helmets. This followed the staging of the dramatic operas, The Ring of the Nibelung (*Der Ring des Nibelungen*) by German composer Richard Wagner in the 1870s, in which its villains wore helmets with horns. It appears this depiction is likely a romanticized creation of modern folk rather than a true depiction of a past culture.

Weapons

A variety of weapons appear from the Viking era, though of course, not everybody had everything. Most Vikings likely did have an ax or a knife, common tools of the time, or another sort of cutting device.

While these items could technically be used to harm or kill, they were not generally utilized in this way. Only warriors and hunters possessed objects like swords, spears and bows to assist them in their roles.

Spears were the weapon of choice for Vikings. The most skilled warriors were said to be able to leap into the air, pluck a spear out of its trajectory and hurl it back into enemy ranks. These throwing spears measured roughly 6.5 feet (2 m) in length. Thrusting spears were longer at about 10 feet (3 m). Imagine the brute strength and skill needed to wield in battle a wooden pole nearly twice one's height!

The battle-ax was another weapon favored by many Vikings. Larger and heavier than regular axes, some of the most famous Viking warriors in history were notorious for their skilled use of these.

Swords were uncommon among Viking warriors, as they were expensive and hard to come by. They were often family heirlooms, passed down through generations. Having a sword was a privilege of the wealthy and prestigious.

Round shields lined with leather for padding and reinforcement were used as protection. Made from a soft wood, the shield was mildly flexible upon impact and often caused enemy weapons to become jammed within. Vikings could then yank the shield away, taking the weapon with it, leaving their adversary unable to attack. The shields could be painted with bright colors and patterns, perhaps to signify a warrior's identity or loyalty.

Although images of Viking war hammers are somewhat popular, there is insufficient evidence of their use in the Viking age.

A Viking warrior group associated with the bear, Berserkers (from Old Norse roots meaning "bear shirt") were said to wear the skins of bears and demonstrate an energetic frenzy in battle. Their notoriety would eventually give rise to the English word "berserk." Their altered state may have derived from stimulants from local plants applied to the fur-lined edges of their shields, which they were known for chewing upon before battle.

Weapons were not only useful items but also a display of wealth and status within the community. Hence, Vikings were often buried with their weaponry.

Makeup

Both men and women wore makeup. Dark coloring around the eyes has been noted, whether as an eyeliner or a dark powder or paste. Such cosmetics could derive from the black henbane plant, the mineral kohl or a number of other natural substances. By darkening the area around the eye, less light is reflected into it, thereby reducing glare when at sea or in the snow.

But makeup didn't have to be purely for practical purposes. A Spanish Arab who visited the Danish market town of Hedeby claimed that Vikings wore makeup to look younger and more attractive. He stated (Kimberleigh Roseblade, 2014):

"There is also an artificial make-up for the eyes, when they use it beauty never fades, on the contrary it increases in men and women as well."

Some Vikings also had a habit of filing grooves into their front teeth and staining them red. This was possibly done to invoke fear or to merely draw the eye to the mouth.

Hair Styles

Long hair in Norse society was possibly thought to grant its owner special powers and was common among both Viking men and women. Hairstyles, however, varied from region to region due to changing fashions and climates.

Braids and knots were popularized by common people who needed to keep their hair and beards tied up for practical reasons but still wanted to remain fashionable. Older Vikings usually tied their hair at the base of the skull and left it at that.

Iron and silver beads were often added to the hair for further adornment.

Men
Men wore their hair in a variety of styles and lengths. Long hair was usually tied back or braided in intricate patterns.

One popular style, witnessed in sculpture and other arts, is known as the reverse mullet. Featuring hair cut shorter in the back and longer in front, it was fashionable among younger men of the tribe.

Women

Women typically wore their hair long, in braids and knots to the back or side. These braids may have been decorated with colored tape or ribbon.

One style popular among young women was called the Valkyrie knot, often depicted in murals of Valkyries, with the hair gathered in a knot at the middle of the back of the head, the loose end flowing downward.

Artwork

When we think of art, Vikings may not be the first people that come to mind. But they had a clear interest in aesthetics that wove its way into their everyday lives in both functional and purely ornamental ways. Beauty was important to Norse life and their engravings, for example, are some of the most intricate and finely detailed in history.

Utilitarian items like brooches, cups, ships and even support columns in buildings were known to be expertly crafted to show beauty and intrigue to the viewer.

Viking art is known for its use of symbolism, as is often seen in other Pagan-based cultures. Abstract forms were favored over realism.

Intricate patterns and animal motifs appear frequently. These were often combined to create intertwining and weaving designs called Norse knotwork, forming the fundamentals of what we know today as Viking art.

Norse knotwork is sometimes confused with Celtic knotwork, also known as Icovellavna. While Celtic knotwork also involves flowing ribbons of interweaving patterns, Norse knotwork features additional designs like animals, nature, and other mythological components. These elongated, abstract animal forms often had simplified and sometimes exaggerated features and limbs.

 The Vikings were master woodworkers, and much of their art revolved around wood carving. However, metals, stone, bones, and even ivory have also been discovered with knotwork engravings.

Textiles were another area for artistic endeavor. Borders on dresses and tunics, clip-on apron panels, embroidery on cloaks, and woven silk endings have all been found with abundant Norse knotwork.

Ships and buildings display plentiful examples of symbolic motifs in Viking art. The Norse often carved the fronts of ships to look like dragons or serpents to scare away bad luck while at sea. Support pillars in homes and communal buildings were covered in ribbons of runes or depicted animals like bears, wolves and eagles, calling on the strength or protection of beasts and gods for additional reinforcement.

Much of Viking artwork revolves around the expression of symbolic meaning in everyday items, whether to convey ideas about social values, mythology or status and influence.

Norse art went through a number of stages over the course of the Viking age and beyond. While other cultures and religions influenced their work, they also managed to maintain distinct traits of their own. The various Norse art styles identified by historians include:

- Oseberg: c. 775–875 AD

- Borre: c. 850–975 AD

- Jellinge: c. 900–975 AD

- Mammen: c. 960s–1025 AD

- Ringerike: c. 990–1050 AD

- Urnes: c. 1050–1125 AD

Oseberg Style

This style of art was named after an oak longship that was found in an early Viking Age burial mound. Being one of the most studied works of the period, the collection of items discovered in the longship—as well as the longship itself—tells us a lot about where Viking artwork began.

Preserved Oseberg ship, photo credits Jean-Pierre Dalbera

This style was vastly popular throughout Scandinavia at the time. It frequently depicted ribbon animals and gripping beasts with mixed geometric patterns. Zoomorphism, the depiction of gods or humans as non-human animals, was very popular, and its use recalled the art's pagan origins.

Oseberg style

Borre Style

The Borre style was another popular method that developed during the Oseberg era. It features many of the same motifs. The ribbon-like forms remain, though with a denser weave, obscuring the background from view. The animal designs were somewhat more realistic and introduced spiral hip joints for many beasts.

The "ring chain" pattern also grew in popularity during this era, consisting of a single ribbon twisting to create a continuous band.

Round brooch, Borre style.

Due to the visual density of this art style, it became very popular in the British Isles and the Baltic Sea. In these areas, delicate compositions were favored, whereas, in other parts of Scandinavia, the style was far more overt.

Jellinge Style

The Jellinge style, while distinctive, is a malleable one. This style was named after a cast silver cup that was found in Jelling, Jutland, in Denmark.

In the Jellinge style, the background is quite visible. The woven patterns are more open and spread out. Depictions of animals and nature are simpler than previous styles but just as prominent. Heads are rounder and less elongated. Eyes are bigger and more obvious. Hip joints, as well as wrist shapes, give more dimension to physical forms. The ribbon animal is still popular; however, the appearance of the gripping beast fades.

Jellinge-style cup, Denmark

The Jellinge style can be found in sites across the world, from the Caspian Sea to the Volga Bulgars, in modern-day western Russia.

Mammen Style

The Mammen style is named after a ceremonial ax that was found in Mammen, Denmark. It was considered a popular style during the reign of King Harald Bluetooth of Denmark and Norway in the later part of the 10th century.

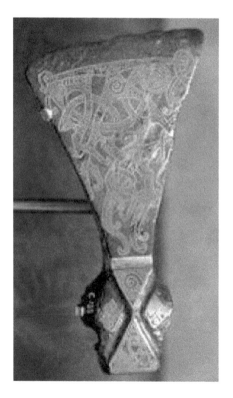

The Mammen Ax, now at the National Museum of Denmark

Long waves and swirls cover the face of the hammers. Nature motifs and exaggerated geometric shapes are used. The Mammen style introduces the Great Beast to the world, as depicted on the Jelling Stone in Denmark. The Great Beast had antlers on its head, a mane around its neck, segmented clawed feet and the body of a serpent. It is said to be a figure that holds great power and influence among the Vikings.

Ringerike Style

The Ringerike style was another highly compacted art form. It obscured much of the background with its tight composure. Double contour lines became popular, and bird figures appeared more frequently. The distinction of note was the common use of the Great Beast imagery and the lack of beaded ornamentation.

Influences from other parts of Europe are evident in this art style, taking inspiration from British and Frankish art techniques. One of these techniques was the inclusion of foliage and tendrils that grew outward from animal bodies, creating beautiful and intricate tangles of nature.

A carved Viking stone slab was discovered in St. Paul's churchyard in London. It is decorated in the Ringerike style. It depicts a Great Beast among long tendrils that curl at their ends. The tendrils wind around the beast, forming horns and a tongue. It also has the spiral hip joint, common to previous art styles, as well as intertwining bodies of beasts. Runic inscriptions on the slab suggest its creator was Swedish.

Ringerike-style ornamentation, from Söderala Kyrka, Söderala, Hälsingland, Sweden

Urnes Style

The last of the art styles to emerge during the Viking Age was known as Urnes, named after a stave church in Urnes, Norway, which bore a clear example of the style.

Urnes Stave Church, image credit: Frode Inge Helland

The Urnes period consisted of three main motifs: a four-legged, regal, standing animal indicative of The Great Beast, a serpent-like creature with one leg (either fore or hind), and thin ribbons. The combination of the three creates beautiful, impactful innovations. The swooping and flowing composition focuses more on symmetry and interlacing designs on a clear background.

Examples of the Urnes style can be found throughout Scandinavia in architecture, runestones and ornaments. In this period, both pagan and Christian iconography were known to be used simultaneously.

Urnes-style deer and snake, photo by Nina Aldrin Thune

Runes

The Vikings were a people who relied more on oral tradition than written documentation. They did not write things down often, but they did, in fact, have a script of their own.

Commonly referred to as runes, the Norse alphabet is a group of symbols that made up the writing system of the Vikings and other Germanic-speaking peoples of Europe in ancient and medieval times. The first known runic inscription dates to 160 AD, with the Vimose comb in Denmark, and runes changed and evolved over the following 1,000 years or so, through the pre-Viking and Viking eras.

Runes were said to have been brought to Midgard by Odin. The poem "Hávamál," from the Poetic Edda, shares that the runes would only reveal their secrets to those it deemed worthy. So Odin set about trying to prove himself. He hung from the branches of the great tree, Yggdrasil, pierced himself with his spear and lived moments from death for nine days and nights. At the end of the ninth night, the runes accepted his sacrifice and divulged their secrets to him.

With this knowledge, he grew much more powerful. He was able to use the runes to create spells for healing the body, easing the mind, binding his enemies, winning love and banishing malevolent forces.

Futharks

There are often two sets of alphabets associated with the Vikings, namely the Elder Futhark and the Younger Futhark. The Elder Futhark was actually in use before the time of the Vikings, from about 160 AD, or earlier, to around 700 AD. It evolved into the Younger Futhark, used in the Viking age beginning around the 700s. As a writing system, runes can be used to convey messages in any spoken language, just as with the Latin alphabet, which we use today to write English and most European languages. However, the runes work best when used for the language of their place and time. For the Vikings, this spoken language is called Old Norse, and the runic alphabet used to write Old Norse during the time of the Vikings was that of the Younger Futhark.

Popular interest in the Elder Futhark today may be due to the fact that, with 24 characters, it can be easier to adapt for modern messages. The Younger Futhark, with 16 characters, uses some letters to represent multiple sounds. The two systems are included below to provide a visual of the letters and how they changed over time. The word "futhark," just like the word "alphabet" for the Latin writing system, derives from its first few characters. Note that as well as denoting a particular sound, each rune also has a name with its own meaning in Old Norse. The rune characters, their roughly corresponding Latin equivalents and the rune names and meanings are all given below.

Elder Futhark

ᚠ (f) *fehu* "fee, cattle"

ᚢ (u) *uruz* "orax (ancient European wild cattle), story, slag"

ᚦ (þ, 'th') *þurisaz* "giant"

ᚨ (a) *ansuz* "one of the Æsir (gods)"

ᚱ (r) *raiðō* "ride, journey"

ᚲ (k) *kaunan* "boil, blister" (possibly "torch")

ᚷ (g) *gebō* "gift"

ᚹ (w) *wunjō* "joy"

ᚺ (h) *hagalaz* "hail" (the precipitation)

ᚾ (n) *nauðiz* "need, emergency, desperation"

ᛁ (I) *īsaz* "ice"

ᛃ (j) *jēra* "year," but typically "harvest, good harvest"

ᛈ (p) *perðō*? "pear tree?" (unclear)

ᛇ (ï/æ?) *eihaz/ei(h)waz* "yew tree" (possibly)

ᛉ (z) *algiz*? "elk"

ᛊ (s) *sōwilō* "sun"

ᛏ (t) *tīwaz/teiwaz* "Týr" (the god)

ᛒ (b) *berkanan* "birch"

ᛖ (e) *ehwaz* "horse"

ᛗ (m) *mannaz* "man"

ᛚ (l) *laguz* "lake" (or possibly "leek")

ᛜ (ŋ, 'ng') *ingwaz* "Ing" (Yngvi, another name of the god Freyr)

ᛞ (d) *dagaz* "day"

ᛟ (o) *ōþala/ōþila* "inherited property, possession"

Younger Futhark

ᚠ (f, v) *fé* "wealth, cattle"

ᚢ (u, w, y, o, ø) *úr* "slag from iron production, rain(storm)"

ᚦ (Þ, ð, 'th') *Þurs* ('thurs') "giant"

ᚬ (o, æ) *áss/óss* "Æsir, estuary" (the Æsir are the main clan of Norse gods)

ᚱ (r) *reið* "ride" (vehicle)

ᚴ (k, g) *kaun* "ulcer, boil"

ᚼ (h) *hagall* "hail"

ᚾ (n) *nauðr* "need, threat, emergency"

ᛁ (I, e) *ísa/íss* "ice"

ᛅ (a, æ) *ár* "year," typically "good year, good harvest"

ᛋ (s) *sól* "sun"

ᛏ (t, d) *Týr* "Týr" (the god, also used for any god)

ᛒ (b, p) *björk/bjarkan/bjarken* "birch"

ᛘ (m) *maðr* "man, person"

ᛚ (l) *lǫgr/lögr* "lake, small body of water"

ᛣ (r) *yr* "yew, yew tree," or possibly "elm"

Uses

Norse runes have a number of different uses, including, naturally, that of documentation. It is, first and foremost, a writing tool. Some of the information we know about Vikings today comes from rune stones, large rocks with engraved lettering that describes mythology, laws or poetry or that commemorates the deceased.

Runes were also included in artwork within the weaving tendrils of patterns. These inscriptions often told tales of Norse myth and legend, linking artwork and history.

Runes may have also been employed in divination. Not to predict the future, necessarily, but rather used as a tool for guidance and insight. Some believe that runic divination was thought to provide the subconscious with something tangible to latch onto or to confirm beliefs that already lay within the heart.

Architecture

Viking architecture is distinctive in its design and function.

New structures were built at every new settlement. These could be temporary or permanent buildings and had to account for the growth and development of the area. The Norse were highly skilled in urban planning.

Evidence from archeological digs shows us that Vikings lived in an organized housing structure within a strategically planned town.

Longhouses

Longhouses were the standard for housing design during the Viking Age. Resembling large upside-down boats, they generally measured about 50 to 72 feet long (15 to 22 meters) and 16 feet wide (5 meters).

They were typically made of wood with clay lining the walls. They had no windows and usually only one entrance. The roof was supported by internal columns, the inside consisting of one large room. These types of longhouses could be found all over Scandinavia. However, places like the Faroe Islands and Iceland, with a scarcity of wood available, show evidence of Viking homes made of sod or turf. Other areas, such as Greenland, used stone in home construction.

It is believed that royals and nobles would paint their houses white. The high visibility of these homes may have functioned as both a symbol of prestige and a useful landmark.

Longhouses usually had a hole in the roof for smoke from the hearth to escape. However, with no windows or full chimneys, Viking homes were likely still quite smoky.

Hard-packed earth over simple stone footings lined the floor of the longhouse. A fire pit at the center served as a communal gathering area where the family could partake in meals, tell tales, perform various tasks and hold meetings.

Cattle, goats and other animals were kept at one end of the longhouse, as well as stored foods, tools and winter gear. The other end could be used for crafts and artisan work.

"Great families" occupied these longhouses, meaning that several generations of a family would live together under one roof. This could get quite crowded but was undoubtedly cozy and helpful in the winter for maintaining heat in the home.

Boathouses

Boathouses were constructed to store boats during winter and when they were not being used. Similar to the longhouse, they measured larger, starting at 82 feet (25 meters) in length, to accommodate the size of the ships being stored. Each vessel received its own enclosure, and multiple boathouses could be built next to each other to house the various boats within a group.

Military Constructions

Being raiders themselves, the Norse knew how best to attack a village and, therefore, how to best protect their villages. They built great circular strongholds surrounding their settlements to shield from enemy attack.

These structures were called Trelleborgs. Similar in design to the circular forts of the Iron Age in Western Europe, they became popular around 980.

The outer walls were lined with trenches. Entryways were situated at each of the four cardinal points. Two main roads joined the gates, meeting in a ring in the middle of town. Residential longhouses were arranged in quadrangles, with merchant stores positioned near the roads.

Religious Buildings

The Norse made use of ritual houses for various community purposes. These consisted of simple wooden buildings with decorative carvings, including on the columns and exteriors. Town artifacts, such as weapons acquired in raids, could be displayed here. Events such as animal sacrifices might take place outside.

Turf Houses

In areas where wood was scarce, turf and stone were used to build homes. A wooden frame was constructed on a bed of flat stones. Turf segments were then affixed to the frame in a herringbone, or zigzag, pattern.

These houses often had highly decorated wooden doorways leading into large halls. A fire would be kept burning in the hearth, providing steady light and warmth.

Icelandic houses also saw the first attached toilets, a convenience likely appreciated at night and during the winter. These were communal, as going to the toilet was seen as a group activity.

Unlike the earthen floors of longhouses, turf house floors were laid in wood or stone, depending on the use of the building and the wealth of its owners.

Ships and Boats

The Vikings were well known for their shipbuilding skills. They created a variety of boats for fishing and merchant trade, as well as warships, riverboats and ferries. Their designs were strong and durable enough to manage the violent winds and frenzied weather of the North Atlantic.

New Technology

Advances in boat making during the 7th and 8th centuries paved the way for a new kind of warship by the Vikings. The development of sails meant that ships could be powered by the wind instead of relying on oars for propulsion.

Combining techniques, the Vikings created vessels that could be propelled by the wind, a rowing crew, or both. They crafted a hull that could handle the force transferred to the frame by the sails and oars. By introducing a keel, the blade that runs the length of the underside of the ship, they gave the ship enough strength and stability to handle the propulsive force.

They also designed a removable mast that could be taken down while the ship was in motion, which, combined with the use of oars, provided greater flexibility, making them less reliant on the wind.

The sail consisted of a large rectangular woolen sheet reinforced by crisscrossed leather bracing. The steering board—the oar used for steering—attached to the ship at the back right side.

Viking ships were said to be fast and strong, surviving crossings of the Baltic and North Seas and even the North Atlantic. Also highly maneuverable, they were able to navigate the shallow waters of inland rivers and bays. This versatility was due in part to having a draft as shallow as 20 inches (50 cm), the draft being the portion of the boat extending below the surface of the water.

Langskip

The langskip was the Viking warship, narrow, long and shallow. Their shape allowed for open spaces perfect for fighting. Both sails and oars were utilized in the langskip for speed and agility.

Knörr

The knörr was a type of merchant ship. Unlike the langskip, it was deep in the draft and more enclosed, focusing on cargo space. Its primary propulsion came from a sail. Knörr ships could be used in instances where fast shipments were required, but this was not frequent.

Clinker-Built Ships

Viking ships were made with the clinker design by riveting overlapping planks together and attaching them to a frame. Spaces between planks were made watertight with a sticky mix of tar or tallow with animal hair, moss or wool.

The overlapping nature of the planks added structure and strength to the ship, allowing the frame itself to be lighter.

This technique created fast, lightweight ships with the aforementioned shallow draft, contributing to ease of mobility in both coastal and inland waters.

After the Viking age, shipbuilding eventually transitioned to using the carvel design. This method called for creating a strong frame first and then attaching planks of any quality wood to the frame. These planks would function simply to keep the water out rather than to contribute to the overall structure and stability of the vessel. These ships tended to be heavier, although the wood required for their construction was also likely easier to source.

Preparation of Timber

Ships were built using simple tools like axes and hammers. The Vikings were known for cutting timber with the grain to produce pieces that maintained strength and flexibility for a low weight. Saws tended to cut against the grain, making for weaker, less flexible planks and were hence not typically used.

Green timber was utilized in the making of ships. "Green" meant that it was used shortly after being felled, as opposed to seasoned wood, which is allowed to dry for several years to produce a hard material. Green wood was pliable and easier to work with, able to bend into complex shapes without splitting or snapping. Cut wood could be stored underwater to maintain its flexibility until it was ready to use.

Oak and pine, the most readily available lumber at the time, were usually used in the construction of Norse boats.

Decoration

Viking ships were known for their elaborate decoration. The stems and sterns were usually carved into the head and body of a water serpent or dragon. These carvings were adorned with bits of metal to enhance their visibility and intimidating appearance from afar.

As we get a better perspective on Viking art and culture, our views of who the Norse were may shift. They become less like mysterious savages and more like multifaceted, real people.

One of the beneficial byproducts of learning about other cultures can be having your views challenged. The next chapter deals with Viking social life, another area with perhaps more surprises in store.

CHAPTER 4

Society in the Nordic Age

Although Vikings have been known as raiders and warriors, they also lived in organized communities, despite what other nations may have thought.

As societies vary with each region, nation, and religion, it is clear the Vikings had social norms all their own. From spiritual beliefs to the handling of slaves and the specific rites of a funeral, the Vikings had their own way of going about their lives. This chapter will outline the distinctive characteristics of typical Viking society.

Religion

In medieval times, almost all humans practiced some kind of worship. The beliefs and practices of the Norse have been called Paganism or Heathenry by others, terms generally used to describe any tradition outside of the major world religions. The Vikings themselves didn't necessarily have a name for their customs. Through their expansion, they were exposed to other belief systems. As time evolved, so too did

Viking religion, with more of them adopting Christian approaches to worship.

For theologists, the Viking Age marks the battle between Christianity and Heathenry and has been studied for many years. The Viking transition from Paganism to Christianity is a complex journey.

Pagan Beginnings

Like many other Pagan societies, the Old Norse religion was polytheistic, meaning that more than one god or goddess was worshiped.

The pagan practices of the Norse were less organized perhaps than that of religions with written texts to adhere to and pass down to others. The Viking people decided how to worship in their own ways, and much of what they knew was passed down through word of mouth and tradition.

Vikings also did not believe in sins and made no attempt at spreading their faith in order to "save others." They believed others were free to worship whomever and however they chose. The few times Vikings opted to repurpose Christian sites and temples as Pagan was more of a military strategy than a religious conquest.

Sacrifice is a frequent theme in historical Paganism and appears in Norse practice as well. In Viking society, it was common to sacrifice cows, chickens, and even dogs as offerings to the gods. Sacrifices could take place prior to a ship voyage, marriage, birth or funeral. At certain events and festivals, slaves could sometimes also be sacrificed. This practice was most customary at the funerals of wealthy chiefs, who were buried with their slaves so as to have aid in the afterlife.

The Influence of Christianity

Vikings were aware of Christianity prior to the first raids. Anglo-Saxon missionaries traveled to Scandinavia in 725 to spread the word of Christianity. While they were welcomed, the religion did not appeal to many of the Viking people, and the mission was therefore deemed a failure.

A second wave of missionaries, supported by the Frankish Emperor Louis the Pious, arrived in Scandinavia in the year 820. Ansgar, Archbishop of Hamburg-Bremen, made his way to Denmark and Sweden. Again, the effort had little impact.

The Vikings came across Christianity once again in their initial raids through the British Isles, Novgorod in western Russia, and Constantinople. By the time the Vikings began their raids, Christianity was already the orthodox religion across much of Europe.

Many of the areas they first raided, such as Lindisfarne, were Christian establishments. Some might think the Vikings were targeting Christians specifically, in moral opposition to them or to promote their own beliefs. However, evidence shows the Norse were not particularly concerned with who followed what system. Rather, monasteries and churches were troves of art, gold, weapons and valued scriptures. These sites were often visited by royalty and upper classes to display their wealth and demonstrate their piety. They were also poorly guarded, making them easy targets for the Vikings. The Norse did not oppose Christians; they merely saw their establishments as easy pickings.

The Vikings discovered that they could hold the items found in these monasteries for ransom, forcing locals to pay to retrieve their precious artifacts and manuscripts. This increased the Vikings' profits and further decreased their overall popularity.

While the Viking conversion to Christianity took time, its advancement was somewhat spurred on by regional trade customs. In many cases, Christian traders would not trade with non-Christians. This began the age of *primsigning*, or "the first signing," in which Vikings would be marked with the cross as a preliminary or halfway point to full baptism and accepting Christianity. This was a popular choice among trading settlements, allowing the Norse to trade with whomever they pleased as long as they wore a cross around their necks.

Traders could then return to wearing the hammer upon return home. Being polytheistic, it was not hard for the Norse to welcome other gods into their traditions alongside their own.

Even so, full conversion was still not a popular practice among Vikings. This eventually began to change, however. As Christian forces began to win more battles, they earned the respect of the Vikings. The Vikings began to see value in their religion and to convert more openly.

The biggest push for conversion, however, came from interaction with the Byzantine Empire. Around the late 9th century, Swedish Vikings and the Kievan Rus state (in modern-day eastern and northern Europe) began fighting for Constantinople.

Constantinople was one of the largest cities the Vikings had ever encountered. With a greater population than Sweden, it was known to be a highly modern and beautiful city. Constantinople also had one of the first naval forces that was able to withstand Viking attacks. Impressive to the Norse people, it inspired many to adopt the Christian tradition.

Another big move toward Christianity was made by King Harald Bluetooth around 965. Runestones documenting this conversion can be found in Denmark. It is stated that King Harald declared all the Danes to be Christian during his rule.

While this was the official position of the country, the real shift happened gradually, both before and after this period.

As more and more Vikings converted to Christianity, it became harder to be a Pagan. Stricter rules arose regarding the attendance of church, baptism, marriage and burials. Blending the two paths or upholding certain Pagan practices proved to be more difficult with time.

Change of Traditions

This transitional era saw the changing of many customs within the Viking community. Vikings were now required to attend weekly mass. They had to profess belief in only one god in order to be baptized.

One feature of this period is that we begin seeing fewer graves with grave goods in them, demonstrating the transition from Pagan to Christian burial practices. Archeologists mark this as a time when a religious shift truly took hold.

Newborns were no longer allowed to be left outside to the elements unless they suffered a distinctive, severe deformation.

The consumption of horsemeat was seen as a pagan practice and was decreed forbidden by Christian leaders. Horses had been a somewhat sacred animal in Norse tradition, appearing in mythology as with Odin's eight-legged horse,

Sleipnir. Horsemeat was occasionally enjoyed, whether for celebration, ritual or as simply another food source. Its consumption in medieval Europe gradually declined with the new laws.

The Vikings had a host of new rules to live by. Most decided to incorporate them into their existing habits. Only a few completely abandoned their old faith for the new.

When Denmark became Christian, many Vikings still practiced Pagan worship in secret or cleverly masked under the guise of Christianity. Many practiced pluralism, the act of acknowledging both religions as being true. A number of Vikings wore both crosses and Thor's hammer about their necks. Crosses have been discovered in the same graves as hammer amulets.

Some transition events were more aggressive. Frankish Emperor Charlemagne forced thousands of Pagans from mainland Europe to Egypt to convert to Christianity at sword-point. Sacred oak groves were destroyed and Pagan symbols torn down.

As times passed, Viking Christians appeared involved in more converting than anyone else. A number of Viking kings and spiritual leaders declared their kingdoms as Christian, including Olaf Tryggvason, Olaf the Stout ("Saint Olaf"), and Magnus the Good.

Iceland likewise felt the momentum of religious change around them and its effect on trade and other business with neighboring kingdoms. Their parliament voted to become Christian in the year 1000.

Some members of the church tried to convince the Pagan Vikings that Norse gods were lesser beings—basically demons. This was not well-received as the Norse gods were such a strong link to their ancestors and integral to their cultural identity.

It is important to note that Christianity did not end the Viking Age, nor did it stop Vikings from being Vikings anymore. Christian Vikings were common and among the most brutal warriors the world had seen. They continued their raids, feuds, enslaving and exploratory expeditions as before.

 In fact, many Viking warriors had their greatest impact after they converted. Harald Hardrada, Amlaib Cuaran, Sytric Silkenbeard, Leif Erikson and Cnut the Great are some of the few Viking leaders who fought while Christian.

The end of the Viking Age saw almost a full conversion of Vikings to Christianity. They were baptized, confessed belief in one god, went to church, and were buried without cremation. Christianity became the gateway for the Norse to expand their reach into the wider world.

Class System

As with most cultures, Norse society had a hierarchy of social classes. At the bottom were found the slaves or thralls, proceeded by the karls, the jarls and finally, the royalty. However, within the Viking class system, individuals were not confined to their class interminably. They had the opportunity to move up or down depending on their actions and luck.

The sagas claim that the first humans created, Ask and Embla, were slaves. The Rígsþula tale accounts how, as more humans populated the earth, the god Heimdall traveled to Midgard, disguised as Rig, and sorted people into their classes.

Thralls

Thralls were the slave class of the Viking society. Being in the lowest social tier meant for a hard, though common, life. Slavery was normal not only for the Vikings but for most of Europe at the time. The populations the Vikings raided, many already thousands of years old, had established and profitable slave trades.

Slaves were at the mercy of their owners. They did not have rights as they were considered "unfree servants." Marked by the collar they wore around their necks and their short hair, they wore plain, undyed clothing and were often barefoot. They were also referred to with gender-neutral pronouns.

Slaves were an important commodity in the Viking Age. While they were primarily acquired through raids and expeditions, the Norse also enslaved their own kind. You could become a slave as a means of punishment for certain extreme crimes, including murder, thievery and high debt.

Children born to slaves were owned by their parents' masters. Killing another's slave required providing a slave as replacement or becoming one yourself to fill the spot until the debt was paid.

A slave could earn their freedom by purchasing their current worth from their owners. This was often difficult to do as it was dependent on the amount of freedom given by their masters. For instance, some slaves were allowed to make and sell baskets in their spare time or grow and sell herbs. Owners could also optionally decide to grant slaves their freedom if they had been a good worker.

Most of the time, slaves were bound to servitude their whole lives, following their masters to the grave. Frequently sacrificed upon the death of their owner, slaves were then included in the burial to follow their master into the afterlife.

Karls

The karls were the working class of the Viking Age. Most Norse fell into this category. One tier above the thralls, these workers were free people and the Old Norse word *"karl"* translates as "free man."

Most of these "freemen" were farmers. Farms were either self-owned or rented from a larger plot owned by another. Other karl occupations included craftsmen, artisans, traders, fishermen, boat builders and soldiers. As much of a karl's work involved manual labor, many of them owned or rented slaves to assist with their trades.

Unlike the slave class, karls were protected by the law and had rights of their own.

The karls also had other duties, such as pledging allegiance to the local jarls, the noble and next-higher class of Norse society. Not only responsible for their own welfare, karls were also obligated, if called upon by the local jarl, to fight or labor for them. Additionally, karls paid taxes to the jarl in the form of money or a percentage of their harvests.

Jarls

The noble class of Viking society, jarls (pronounced "yarls" with a "y" sound as in "yarn"), were akin to the local chiefs and village elders. They rose to their position either through election by the karls or by acquiring power through riches or force.

The jarls owned large plots of land, including property they rented out to karls to farm for them. They had much money and influence within society. They governed the local community, making decisions on various issues.

The jarls were the war leaders who often led raids funded by their own money. They influenced karls to join their raids by calling upon allegiances or promising small cuts of the treasure.

Jarls were all trained in combat from an early age and made up some of the best fighters and strategists in the military ranks. Owing to their wealth and acquisitions, they also had access to the best weapons and armor, even occasionally swords.

Royals

The royals were the highest social class of the Vikings. They were few and far between as the presence of kings and queens in Norse society developed gradually over time. The Vikings initially lived in small clans run by the local jarl chieftain.

As these jarls obtained more power and influence fueled by their conquests, they began to extend their rule to other clans, giving rise to a new class of kings and queens. Jarls under the rule of the royals were then pledged to aid during battle with warriors and taxes sourced from their own clans.

Kings and queens had great power. They were able to gather huge armies and plan massive raids on foreign lands, even upon those with substantial armed forces. This was the beginning of Viking-run territories becoming unified countries, as multiple clans were brought together.

Treatment of Women

Evidence has suggested that Viking women had many more rights than other women of their time. They benefited from more freedoms and held greater influence over their households and communities than in other parts of the world.

Even so, Norse women still experienced limitations. They could not speak in court or receive a man's inheritance. Men maintained political power. But women were granted control in other areas.

Female entrepreneurs were common in the Viking Age. Arts, crafts, and textiles were made and sold by the women of the villages. They managed their own businesses and profits and were not required to give their earnings to their husbands or families. Many of their businesses were lucrative and successful.

Women were also in charge of household finances and were often seen to be the managing force behind a household. They were respected for their roles in society. They could buy and own land and were usually responsible for managing the properties belonging to the family.

Women were solely responsible for housework and food preparation. Much of their time was taken up by household chores, and thus most Norse women were skilled in spinning, woolworking, sewing, weaving, cooking, gathering and animal care. Children and the elderly were also cared for by women.

During times of war, women solely ran the villages, with most of the men gone to battle. Trade, farming and commerce never declined during these times, demonstrating the Viking woman's proficiency in running estates.

Women also had control over their own marital fates. While arranged marriages were popular, women had the right to refuse suitors. They could also divorce their husbands if they so wished, a practice unique to Viking women. Their dowries would then be returned to them, allowing them to begin their lives anew. Divorced or widowed women could remarry without shame, and it was, in fact, encouraged in Viking society.

There are also tales of women warriors or shield-maidens, although their frequency may be debated. Female explorers and settlers also arise in the sagas. The great explorer Gudrid Thorbjarnardóttir crossed the North Atlantic with some of the first Europeans to settle in North America, in the region they dubbed Vinland on the eastern shores of modern-day Canada. Another traveler, Aud the Deep-Minded, prominent in the settlement of Iceland, also commanded her own fleet.

Households

Households were considered "headed" by men but run by women. A woman's role centered around the family, the farm and the household. When men were away at battle, women became the sole leaders of the household.

Children belonged to the household of their parents until they married. The wife would then either move into the husband's household, or the couple would break off to start their own.

As mentioned earlier, it was common for Viking households to house "grand families" where several generations of extended family lived under the same roof. The elderly would move in with their children when they became too old to look after themselves.

Marriage

Vikings married young. Women were usually married between the ages of 12 and 15, and men married before they were 20. Marriages were also often arranged for financial or social benefit. Many were arranged so as to create new alliances or end old feuds.

Unlike other cultures around the world, Viking men and women shared marriage duties almost evenly. Once they were married, they were responsible for each other. Each had a role to fill, or they could risk divorce—another unique trait of Viking marriages.

Marriage was important to Viking society as people were expected to reproduce to ensure the longevity of their civilization.

There were two stages to getting married: the betrothal and the wedding. The betrothal was more socially significant, establishing the terms of commitment to one another, whereas the wedding was purely ceremonial.

Betrothal

The betrothal was a legally binding contract, handled like a business deal, with both parties signing their consent. Dowries were discussed and agreed upon. Money swapped hands and gifts were exchanged. Both families became invested in the union and could not go back on their word without incurring financial loss.

Wedding planning could take up to three years while the families settled financial matters like dowries, property transfers and inheritances.

Wedding

Once the financial matters were solved, a public wedding ceremony and grand feast were held. These parties usually lasted a few days and could sometimes go on for a whole week, depending on the wealth of the couple's families.

Weddings were usually held on a Friday to honor Frigg, the goddess of marriage and fertility. Autumn was the preferred season for marriage, being associated with abundance. The fresh harvest ensured there was enough to feed the wedding celebrants.

During the ceremony, the groom would present the bride with a familial sword, which she would take with the intention of giving it to her future son. The bride's father would present the groom with a sword to signify the transfer of guardianship of the woman to her new husband. This sword was thrust into the support column of the couple's new home. The depth of the cut represented the success of the marriage.

The bride and groom exchanged rings, much like modern wedding ceremonies today. Brides wore wreaths of flowers around their heads. Grooms were decorated with swords and weapons.

An event called the *brud hlaup* followed the wedding ceremony. The families of the newlyweds would participate in a foot race in the reception hall. The losing family would serve the ale for the feast.

A month's worth of sweet ale brewed from honey was typically gifted to the bride and groom on the eve of their wedding. A toast was raised to Odin and Frigg to bless the union between the couple and aid them in getting pregnant. This Norse tradition hence gave rise to the term *honeymoon*.

The last custom of Viking marriages involved the wedding party escorting the bride and groom to their bedroom, ensuring they climbed into bed together before leaving. Likely to celebrate procreation, but also perhaps marital intimacy, this was a common practice across the world in those times.

Divorce

One distinction between Norse culture and other regions of the world during the Viking age was the ability of Viking women to divorce their husbands. This could be on the grounds of failing finances, domestic violence and even poor sexual performance. Male infidelity, however, was not a cause for divorce.

While men could have multiple romantic partners, women were required to remain faithful throughout their marriage. Men's mistresses could even live with them in the same household, though the wife maintained authority over these women.

The consequences of adultery for married women were severe. Divorce was needed before she could be with another man.

It is interesting to note that only women could petition for divorce. There is no written evidence that a man could divorce a woman.

Once a woman declared divorce, she was entitled to financial compensation in addition to the return of her family's dowry. This would allow the newly free woman to live comfortably on her own until she found another husband or until old age if she preferred. Small children and babies usually went with the woman. Older children could be divided up, going to live with either family.

Birth and Children

Procreation was the duty of any married couple. Childbirth was a sacred and critical time for any family.

Mothers usually gave birth in the home. Pregnant women would cease all travels beyond the home for the last month of pregnancy. The father would also stop all travels and remain in the village with his wife. It was tradition for a father to be present with the wife at the time of birth.

Women usually gave birth in a squatting or kneeling position on the ground. In the event that she had to lie on her back, she was raised off the floor by a chair or a bare bed.

After the birth, the mother and child were bathed before the mother could receive the baby for the first time and nurse it. Everyone present at the birth would witness this.

Nine days after the baby was born, a ceremony called *vatni ausinn* would be held. The baby was placed on the knee of the kneeling father and sprinkled with water. It would then be presented with its name for the first time.

Naming was important to Vikings. They believed names held great power and significance in how a person's life would turn out. Children were often named after ancestors, as the Vikings believed in reincarnation. Names could come from gods or other mythic origins. Infants were also named after current or desirable traits.

After the naming ceremony, the baby became an official member of the household. They were expected to fulfill their role in the family and were entitled to an inheritance. Once they were older—typically around age 12 to 14—they would have a say in household affairs and management. Children remained part of the household until they married, at which point they would be seen as an adult.

One interesting aspect of Viking society was the handling of children with birth defects. If a child showed any signs of deformity or disability—or in the case of extreme poverty where the parents could not afford to take care of the child— the parents might toss it down a well or leave it to the elements. In such a physically demanding society, this was seen as both practical and more merciful than forcing the child to live a life of hardship.

As we saw earlier, the introduction of Christianity greatly limited this practice, with the exception of children with strong deformities.

Viking society was a structured affair. It ran by a set of distinct rules, and each person knew their role within it. While we can argue the ethicality of their society, we cannot deny its straightforward approach.

The next chapter will demonstrate how that approach aided many Vikings in making a name for themselves.

CHAPTER 5
Famous Nordic Warriors

Fighting Culture

Some of the most famous Vikings were warriors and conquerors. They were highly skilled in close combat (using, for example, fists, axes and the thrusting of spears) and ranged combat (with bow and arrow and throwing stones or spears). It was said that if you were a true warrior and died on the battlefield, you were chosen to join Odin in his hall of the dead, Valhalla, an admirable outcome for any Viking combatant.

Vikings were known for their swift, unannounced attacks and raids. They were skilled in reconnaissance work. Known to be efficient in their assaults, they targeted critical defenses first. Their strategies led to success in most of their raids.

Warrior Groups

Each clan had its own warrior group. Some smaller groups functioned under a larger banner when needed, but otherwise, they worked independently of each other. There were, however, a few notable groups that emerged during the Viking Age.

The Berserkers

The berserkers were the fiercest and wildest of Viking warriors. They fought in a trance-like state, seemingly immune to pain. They focused solely on destroying what was before them.

This frenzied state could sometimes be problematic as they were known to hack away at whoever crossed their path, unable to recognize friend from foe. It could become dangerous to place them too close together, lest they kill each other by accident.

These Vikings wore the skins of wolves and bears as a mark of their clan and an omen to strike fear into their enemies. They were said to have howled and foamed at the mouth in their frenzies.

After a few hours, the berserkers would calm down into a feeble, disoriented state.

Scholars believe that certain drugs may have been used to induce their trance. These substances include a mushroom called Fly Amanita (Amanita muscaria) and the plant Henbane (Hyoscyamus niger). They postulate that the berserkers would soak the furry edges of their shields in mixtures of the drugs and suck on them before and during battle.

The Varangian Guard

The Varangian Guard was created in 988 when Vladimir I of Kyiv sent Byzantine Emperor Basil II six thousand Norse warriors from his own troops to aid Constantinople in battle. Vladimir was gifted Basil's sister, Anna, as a wife in return. These Norse immigrants were what the eastern Romans termed "Varangians," and they hailed originally from Sweden mostly, with some from Denmark and Norway.

The Varangian Guard lasted well into the 14th century. They were composed of the best and most loyal fighters and formed the personal bodyguard for the Byzantine Emperors and their families. They also served as the local police force of Constantinople.

While the Varangian Guard was initially composed of Viking raiders, they became more diverse over the years, encompassing Anglo-Saxons, Normans and others in their ranks.

The Guard served the title of emperor rather than the individual emperor. If the throne was taken by force, their loyalties would shift to the new ruler.

They earned the nickname "The Emperor's Wineskins" for their habit of frequenting pubs and brothels, getting drunk and causing trouble.

The Varangian Guard fought in many battles and was known for their brutal fighting style, using swords and battle axes. They preferred fighting on foot despite their excellent horse-riding skills.

Shield-Maidens

Shield-maidens are a much-debated concept in Norse mythology. Shield-maidens were female Vikings who accompanied the men into battle, fighting alongside them as equals.

While this may have been uncommon, recent evidence shows us that they did exist.

In the 1800s, archeologists uncovered a grave of a respected Viking warrior. They were buried with "grave goods" typical to warriors of the time: a sword, an ax, shields, two horses, armor-piercing arrows and a strategy game. This demonstrated that the warrior had held great influence in the society, was reasonably wealthy and was a strategist.

As was common for the time, the body was assumed to be male.

It was only in 2017 that DNA analysis of the bones showed the warrior to be female. This changed the way we perceive Viking women and their roles in society. Prior to this discovery, shield-maidens were assumed to be purely mythological.

Famous Vikings

Not all Vikings stood the test of time. Chiefs, warlords and warriors alike, most Vikings were lost to history. The few stories that remain show how distinctive the Norse could be. Vikings became famous for many things, namely feats of strength and conquests.

Rollo of Normandy

Rollo (c. 860 -930) was a Viking chief who became the first King of Normandy. He was known for converting to Christianity in 911 as part of a deal with Frankish king Charles the Simple. He instituted Christianity as the religion of Normandy.

Erik the Red

Erik the Red (Erik Thorvaldsson) is one example of the Norse fighters' bloodthirsty nature. A 10th century warrior, he was named after the bright red color of his hair. He was banished from Iceland for murdering several people and ended up discovering and founding Greenland in the process.

Freydis Eiriksdottir

Freydis Eiriksdottir is the daughter of Erik the Red. Just as brutal as her father, she helped him settle Vinland in North America.

The sagas tell of a story when their encampment was attacked by locals, and she flew into a fit of madness, driving away the natives single-handedly with only a sword. Perceiving her as some kind of demon, they ran off. Even more impressive is that she achieved this while eight months pregnant!

She also successfully ran her own trading scheme. Her key to obtaining more profits was to kill her existing partners so her share became larger.

Leif Erikson

Leif Erikson is the son of Erik the Red and brother to Freydis Eiriksdottir. He is credited with traveling to North America along with his father and sister a full five hundred years before Christopher Columbus. They arrived in the year 1000 after they accidentally veered off course en route to Greenland. He returned with more Vikings to establish a settlement in what is now thought to be Newfoundland, Canada. The Norse name for the area, Vinland, meaning "land of wine," comes from the plentiful grapes that grew wild there and the delicious wines they made, a privileged drink in Norse culture.

Ragnar Lothbrok

Ragnar Lothbrok was a forceful Viking warrior who led many successful raids during the 9th century. His attacks on Francia and Anglo-Saxon England gave him legendary status.

He earned the nickname "Shaggy Breeches," after the woolen pants he was known to wear.

He was rumored to have fought a dragon and survived.

His invasion of England, which he led with just two ships, proved unsuccessful and led to his death.

Bjorn Ironside

Bjorn Ironside was the son of Ragnar Lothbrok and a well-known Viking leader. He was most famous for the raids he led on France and the Mediterranean Sea in the 9th century.

Customary with the Vikings, as the youngest son, Bjorn was cast out and forced to make a life for himself. He ended up raiding West Francia, the Iberian coast and much of the Mediterranean, including countries such as England, France, and Italy.

To his enemies, he appeared unstoppable. He eventually returned home after the death of his father and became King of Sweden.

Ivar the Boneless

Son of Ragnar Lothbrok, Ivar the Boneless was named for his bone condition. He had a disease that gave him brittle bones that broke easily. His feats were hence that much more impressive.

He was a berserker who led his fellow warriors through numerous victories. His fame centers upon his invasions of several Anglo-Saxon kingdoms in the 9th century.

Halfdan Ragnarsson

Another son of Ragnar Lothbrok, Halfdan Ragnarsson led The Great Army that helped his brother, Ivar the Boneless, invade Northumbria, England in 865. The kingdom was placed under their control.

Gunnar Hamundarson

Gunnar Hamundarson was known to be a formidable swordsman and amazing jumper. It was said that he could leap higher than he was tall, even in full body armor. He was a skilled archer and stone thrower, unusual skills even among warriors.

A savage fighter, he raided the coasts of Denmark and Norway during the 10th century.

Eric Bloodaxe

Eric Bloodaxe (Eric Haraldsson) was the prince of Norway. Born to King Harald Fairhair, he was raised as a ruthless

Viking warrior. He began participating in raids with his father's army at the age of 12.

He earned the nickname 'Bloodaxe' after murdering all but one of his brothers. This placed him in line to inherit the throne after his father died. Eric Bloodaxe was known as being a firm and unyielding king, unpopular with the masses and ruling with oppression and force. He was later forced to give up the throne to his remaining brother.

Olga of Kyiv

Olga of Kyiv was the Viking princess of Kievan Rus in the 10th century. She is most famous for becoming a saint after she took revenge on the tribe that killed her husband, the Grand Prince Igor I.

Olga was Varangian and was trained in combat and strategy. She was 15 years old when she married Igor and 20 when he was murdered.

As her three-year-old son, Sviatoslav, was too young to rule, Olga became regent of Kievan Rus. Using her newfound power and resources, she burned her enemies alive, buried diplomats that tried to appease her, and destroyed their towns in retribution for her husband.

She converted to Christianity during her rule. In 1547, the Russian Orthodox Church recognized her as an official saint, the patron saint of widows and converts.

Harald Hardrada

Harald Hardrada was known as a ferocious warrior with a hard approach to leadership and discipline. His ruling methods were considered aggressive and inflexible. Becoming King of Norway in 1046, he led a surprisingly peaceful reign and is regarded as one of the last great Viking kings.

He died getting shot in the neck at the Battle of Stamford Bridge in England, where his troops were taken by surprise and attacked by the army of King Harold Godwinson.

Cnut the Great

Cnut (or Canute) is the son of King Svein Forkbeard of Denmark. He became the sole ruler of England in the early 11th century.

After his father died, the Danish throne was inherited by the Anglo-Saxon king, Aethelred the Unready and then by his son, Edmund Ironside. After Cnut defeated Edmund during the Battle of Ashingdon, he was given a portion of England to rule. When Edmund died, he inherited the rest of the kingdom.

As it turns out, Cnut was a great ruler who brought back stability and peace to the region after years of torment by raids. Through the years, Cnut also acquired control of Denmark, Norway and parts of Sweden.

Hervor

Hervor was a well-known shield-maiden that descended from a long line of berserkers. She was a fierce woman, more interested in learning archery, swordsmanship and horse riding than household chores.

Hervor frequently challenged herself, setting up fights with the boys of her village. When she had beaten all of them, she set out on a pilgrimage of sorts. During this time, she discovered that her father was Angantyr, a berserker chief famous for carrying Tyrfing, the cursed sword of legend.

Believing the sword to be her birthright, she journeyed out to find it. She discovered it in her father's grave on the Island of Samsø. It was rumored that Angantyr took the sword to his grave as it was too powerful and dangerous to wield.

Hervor used the sword for many years, having no issue with it. However, it is said that her sons were driven mad by its power when they tried to use it.

The Vikings were quite successful in their raids and conquests. Both men and women made names for themselves, and their stories continue on in Norse legend. Alongside these stories arise those of the divine warriors as well. Let's take a look at the famed deities of Norse mythology.

CHAPTER 6

Norse Deities

Many people may be familiar with various Norse deities from modern media. We learn of Thor as the god of thunder with his trusty hammer, Mjollnir. We see Loki, a shapeshifting miscreant who toys with the line between hero and villain.

How much of what we see is rooted in historical sources, and how much is the product of modern storytelling? This chapter aims to introduce the gods of the Vikings and their characteristics as interpreted from Norse mythology.

Deity Clans

Norse mythology contains two main clans of deities, namely the Æsir and the Vanir, while some include the Jötnar as a third clan. These groups of beings each play a role in maintaining the balance of the cosmos.

The Æsir were known as the greater gods. They lived in the realm of Asgard and were patrons of the celestial plane, war and natural elements.

The Vanir were minor gods who lived in Vanaheim. They were bound to the earthly plane and practiced magic. They were the gods of harvest, fertility, wealth and the seas. These gods were popular among the working class.

The Jötnar were beings of chaos who lived in Jotunheim or Jötunheimr (pronounced YOT-un-haim/YOT-un-haim-ar). Wild with magic and power, they are often referred to as giants, though their actual size can vary. They were the natural enemies of the Æsir and Vanir, even though many of these were part Jötunn (the singular of Jötnar) themselves.

Æsir-Vanir War

The art of *seidr* was a form of powerful magic performed by the Vanir. The goddess Freya was the first practitioner of the craft and would often venture from place to place, offering her skills for hire.

Disguised under the name Heiðr, she finally visited Asgard. The Æsir were immediately mesmerized by her talents and eagerly sought her power. They began to sweep aside their morals of honor, loyalty and kinship in exchange for more selfish pursuits.

They eventually realized the folly of their ways and blamed it on Freya, calling her Gullveig, translating to "gold-greed." They attempted to murder her, but with her powers, she was reborn. Three times they burnt her alive; three times she rose from the ashes.

Fear rising in the Æsir ranks, the Asgardians banished Freya from their realm. Hostilities grew on both sides until it erupted into all-out war. The Æsir fought by means of physical combat and brute force, while the Vanir retaliated with magic.

The war endured for some time, each side having their turn to temporarily sway the fight to their advantage. However, the longer the battle wore on, the more it became clear that they were evenly matched.

Eventually, both the Æsir and the Vanir became tired of fighting and decided to call a truce. As was customary in Norse tradition, tribute was paid by each side. Njord, Freya and Freyr were sent by the Vanir to live in Asgard. Hoenir and Mimir were sent by the Æsir to live in Vanaheim.

Gods and Goddesses

Individual gods and goddesses in Norse mythology each had their own special traits, skills and areas of influence. The connection of the Norse people with any particular god at any time might have to do with events occurring at the moment, assistance required for certain deeds, a familiar or clan association with a particular deity or simply the time of year or the current whim of the individual or group. The Norse had an abundance of varied deities on which to call at any given time.

Odin

Odin was the father of the gods, known as the "Allfather." The god of wisdom, war, poetry and death, he was the ruler of Asgard and the leader of the Æsir. He is said to be unmatched in cunning and battle prowess. He led the Æsir in the battle against the Vanir.

He is depicted as a strong man with a long flowing beard and only one eye. Legend tells that he tore out his right eye and drank from the god Mimir's body in order to gain unparalleled wisdom.

Odin was a strong shapeshifter. His preferred forms were eagles, snakes and other powerful creatures. He was also known to pose as a traveler and visit the earthly realm of Midgard to stir up trouble.

He had two ravens, Huginn and Munin, who traveled the world listening and reporting back what they had seen to Odin. They could often be found sitting on his shoulder and whispering into his ear. Stories reflect that Odin is often more interested in them than members of his own court.

Odin also had two wolves, Geri and Freki, as familiars. They would follow him into battle, eating the corpses of his enemies.

Odin learned the magical arts of *seidr*, which gave the user the ability of foresight. As such, Odin was known to be able to see the future as well as the spirits of the dead.

In imagery, he is often depicted with his staff or spear and seated upon Hlidskjalf, the high throne from which he could see each of the nine realms.

Thor

Thor is Odin's son and is said to be the fiercest warrior who ever lived. Known as the red-haired god of thunder, Thor is marked as the protector of the realms of Midgard and Asgard and was highly worshiped and regarded among the Vikings. Known for his strength and bravery, he loved fighting and would never pass up an opportunity to show off his skills.

Thor's famous war hammer, Mjollnir (pronounced "MYULE-near"), is known for being an iconic symbol of Norse mythology, meaningful to both Vikings of old and Norse pagans and other enthusiasts today. While the hammer was strong, it was not the source of Thor's power; it was rather an extension of himself. It did have some interesting qualities of its own, however, such as being able to return to Thor's hand after being thrown. It could also raise the dead to fight on his behalf.

Thor owned a belt called Megingjörd that claimed to double his power upon use, making him a truly devastating force. He also wore gloves called Járngreipr ("iron grippers"). The hammer, belt and gloves were synonymous with the thunder god.

Though he seldom used it, Thor possessed a staff known as Grídarvölr.

It is written that Thor was destined to kill and be killed by Jörmungandr, the giant sea serpent and son of Loki, at Ragnarök, the prophesied end of days.

Loki

Loki was neither Æsir nor Vanir. He was actually Jötunn and the half-brother of Odin. Due to this connection, he was allowed to live in Asgard. He was known as the god of deception and mischief.

Loki could shapeshift and was known for his flexible loyalty, quick wit and sharp tongue. He is described by Snorri Sturluson in the Gylfaginning of the Prose Edda as "beautiful and comely to look upon, evil in spirit, very fickle in habit."

Trying to decipher Loki's motivations can be quite difficult. As much trouble as he stirred up for the other gods, he provided them aid just as frequently, often helping them talk or trick their way out of shady deals and promises.

His mischief ranged from harmless to extreme. He once cut off all of Sif's hair, the wife of Thor, while she slept. Furious and about to set her husband upon him, Loki revealed he had already convinced the dark elves to make her hair of gold.

On the more severe side, Loki tricked Hodr into slaying Baldr, two sons of Odin, and ran off before he could be punished. In the Æsir's attempt to bring Baldr back from the land of the dead, a giantess, suspected to be Loki in disguise, intervened and thwarted their effort.

Loki was then hunted down and captured. Taken to a cave, he was tied to a rock by the entrails of his son Nari. Skadi, the Jötunn goddess of Winter, suspended a serpent above him so that its venom would fall on Loki's face for all eternity. Loki's wife, Sigyn, was said to remain by his side, catching the poison in a bowl before it could drip onto his face. It was only when she turned to empty the bowl that Loki was burned by the venom. The pain was so intense that Loki's howls and writhing were thought to bring about earthquakes on Midgard.

Loki remains tied to that rock until Ragnarök, when he sails out as commander of the ship of Helheim, the land of the dead, and is fated to be slain at the hands of Heimdall.

Interestingly, Loki was not documented as having any worshippers or rituals dedicated to him. He appears to be the only one of the more commonly depicted gods without a cult following.

Njord

Njord was the god of wind and sea. The patron god of fishermen, sailors and sea traders, he was also the god of justice.

He is the father of many of the Vanir deities. He led the Vanir in the war against the Æsir. He was later sent to Asgard with his children, Freya and Freyr, in accordance with the peace treaty.

Njord was known for his failed marriage with the giantess Skadi. Skadi had come to Asgard to avenge her father's recent death. The Æsir assuaged her by, among other means, offering her a husband in a blind choosing game. All the gods lined up behind a curtain with just their feet and legs showing, and she was asked to select one for her mate. Thinking it was the fair god Baldr, Skadi picked Njord.

It was an unhappy union from the start. Njord, being the god of water, wanted to live in his home, Nóatún ("The Place of Ships"), but Skadi wanted to return to her home in the snowy mountains. For a while, they took turns living at each others' homes before they decided to call it quits and part ways.

Njord eventually sired children with whom many believe to be his unnamed sister.

Unlike most other gods, he is fated to be one of the few who make it out alive at the end of Ragnarök.

Freya

Originally from Vanaheim, Freya (or Freyja) is the daughter of Njord and the twin to Freyr, all three of whom relocated to Asgard following the Æsir-Vanir war. While some say she was the cause of the war, she was quickly accepted into the ranks of the Æsir when she arrived.

Freya is the goddess of love, lust, fertility, and beauty. She is more associated with the fertility of sexuality and childbearing than that of agricultural abundance. Unlike other goddesses of fertility, she is not portrayed as innocent or pure but rather more of a party girl. She was frequently caught fornicating with various beings for favors and manipulation.

As a Vanir, she was skilled in magic and was the first practitioner of the art of *seidr,* which she taught to Odin at his request. Njord and Freya were hence appointed high priest and priestess of sacrificial offerings of Asgard.

Freya was also the mistress of Fólkvangr, a hall of fallen warriors.

She was married to the god Odr, and together they bore a daughter by the name of Hnoss.

Freya loved to travel and had many ways of doing so. She was often seen carried by her cat-drawn chariot. Her falcon feather cloak also received much use and allowed her to fly across realms. She frequently loaned the cloak to other gods, including to Loki for the rescue of the goddess Idunn from Jotunheim.

A third way Freya traveled was with her battle-boar, Hildisvíni. Loki teased that Hildisvíni was actually her lover whom she turned into a boar so that no one could accuse her of being scandalous when she rode him in public.

She is said to be one of the few gods to rise at the end of Ragnarök.

Freyr

The son of Njord and twin to Freya, Freyr is his sister's natural counterpart. He is the patron god of harvest, virility, weddings and wealth. Freyr was thus popular among the Vikings, especially farmers and merchants.

Freyr sailed a magical ship, Skíðblaðnir, that always met favorable winds, no matter where it went. It was said to be foldable, fitting easily into a specially-made bag on his hip. When he was not traveling by ship, he rode his chariot, pulled by a golden boar dubbed Gullinbursti.

Freyr was one of the gods who routinely received ritual sacrifices from the Vikings. Occasions such as weddings or the celebration of a harvest were usually accompanied by the offering of a boar.

Frigg

Frigg is the wife of Odin and the Queen of Asgard. She is the patron goddess of love and marriage. She had a strong cult following in the Viking Age.

Frigg was known to wear a blue cape symbolizing the sky.

She was attributed to giving Baldr, her son, his near-immortality, as told below.

There is some possibility that Freya and Frigg were originally the same entity. Both goddesses of love and practitioners of the magic of seidr, they share other similarities as well. Their names and those of their husbands are quite alike, and both have been credited with having Friday named after them.

Baldr

Baldr is the son of Odin and Frigg. Known as the god of peace, light, beauty and nature, he was well-loved among the gods.

He was killed by his brother Hodr, the god of darkness, by accident. The saga tells of Frigg compelling the beings of the realm to swear not to harm her son. She tracked down every living thing, but for mistletoe, thought to be harmless enough. Frigg returned to relay the good news to her son, Baldr.

To celebrate his newfound immortality, the gods took turns throwing knives, wooden stakes and other weapons at Baldr. They bounced off, leaving him unharmed. Loki, under the guise of helping Hodr join in on the fun, helped the blind god aim an arrow at his brother. What Hodr did not know was that the arrow was fashioned from mistletoe. It pierced Baldr's heart, and he was immediately killed. He then journeyed on to the underworld.

This event was said to mark the beginning of Ragnarök.

Hel

Hel (sometimes called Hela) is the daughter of Loki and the Jötunn Angrboda. She and her two siblings, Jörmungandr, the serpent, and Fenrir, the great black wolf, were prophesied in their early years to be a source of trouble in Ragnarök. In an effort to confine them, Odin dealt with each of them in unique ways. Hel was banished to the land of the dead, which came to be known as Helheim. Considered by some to be the goddess of death, she ruled over the underworld as queen.

Portrayed as a beautiful young girl on one side and a rotting corpse on the other, Hel showed little concern for the dead nor the living. Greedy and cruel, she did not allow anyone to escape her realm.

When Baldr was sent to Hel, the Æsir gods came down to petition for his release. Having the same quick wit as her father, she devised a plan. She promised that she would release Baldr if everyone in Asgard wept for him. Everyone wept except for a giantess called Thökk, who many scholars believe to be Loki in disguise. The deal was left unfulfilled, and Baldr remained in Helheim until the end of Ragnarök.

Vidar

Vidar is the son of Odin and the giantess Gríðr. He was proclaimed the strongest god after Thor, his older half-brother.

One of the few gods to survive Ragnarök, he avenged his father, Odin, after the Allfather was eaten by Fenrir, the great wolf. Wearing a magic shoe made for this purpose, Vidar was said to kick the wolf's jaw open and slash its mouth to pieces, thereby ending its destruction.

Vali

Vali is the son of Odin and the giantess, Rindr. Seemingly born for the sole purpose of avenging his brother Baldr, he is full-grown and ready for the task twenty-four hours after birth. He finds and slays Hodr, Baldr's killer, despite Hodr's role here appearing to be more of a pawn of Loki than a mastermind in his own right.

Tyr

Tyr is one of the oldest gods of Asgard. Known as the god of justice, he was revered among the other deities. He held power over oaths, contracts and peace treaties.

Tyr was known as the one-armed god. As the story goes, the gods were trying to decide how to handle Fenrir, the great black wolf foretold to be a source of future destruction. They commissioned the dwarves to craft an unbreakable chain to ensnare him.

The gods tried to goad Fenrir into being chained up so that he might demonstrate his strength by breaking out. But upon seeing the unusual thing—a delicate chain the gods had laid out—Fenrir hesitated in distrust.

As a show of good faith, Tyr offered his hand to the jaws of Fenrir while the gods fastened the chain around him. When Fenrir discovered that he could not break free of his bonds, he bit off Tyr's arm.

Týsdagr (Tuesday) is named after this god.

Heimdall

Heimdall is an Æsir god known as the guardian of Asgard. Due to his incredible senses, he earned a home at

Himinbjörg, the site in Asgard where the Bifrost bridge stretches toward Midgard, the realm of humanity. Heimdall's keen eyesight allowed him to see for hundreds of miles in both the day and the night. His acute hearing could pick up the sound of grass growing and wool lengthening on the backs of sheep.

Adding to Heimdall's mystique, he was said to be born of nine mothers. Professed to be sisters, some posit they may refer to the nine daughters of the sea deities Ran and Aegir, personified as ocean waves.

Heimdall was the keeper of the Gjallarhorn, a horn that would echo through the heavens and across realms on the day of Ragnarök. He is fated to slay Loki in the apocalypse.

A Note About the Days of the Week

The Romans had titled their days of the week after their gods and corresponding planets and celestial bodies. The romance languages of today, such as Spanish, French and Italian, continue to show these origins. The Germanic people adopted this tradition and found similar gods in their mythology with which to name the days of the week. Through the Germanic roots of English, we can see the links with old Norse deities in our day names, noted below.

Sunday - Sol or Sunna, the goddess of the sun

Monday - Mani, the god of the moon

Tuesday - Tyr, the one-handed god who helped to trap the wolf, Fenrir

Wednesday - Wodin or Odin, head of the Æsir, god of wisdom, magic and much more

Thursday - Thor, the courageous warrior god of thunder, loyalty, strength, honor

Friday - Frigg or Freya, goddesses of love and beauty

The name for Saturday was retained from the Roman day name, attributed to the Roman god Saturn.

Now that we have gained some insight into a number of the principal Norse deities, we can set about exploring where and how they lived. The next chapter will investigate the Nine Realms of the World Tree, how they are connected and how they affect the beings residing within them.

CHAPTER 7

The Nine Realms of Norse Mythology

The people of ancient Nordic culture had envisioned a universe of nine distinct worlds or realms, held together and connected by the World Tree, known as Yggdrasil. Within these realms, they placed certain gods, humans and creatures, and each realm had its own particular physical environment.

The World Tree

Yggdrasil, the World Tree, joins the nine realms together. Its evergreen branches reach high into the heavens, and its roots extend deep into the spiritual waters running beneath it: the spring of Hvergelmir and the wells of Mímisbrunnr and Urðarbrunnr.

The roots of the tree are watered from Urðarbrunnr by the Norns, three female entities who spin threads of fate. Four stags, Dáinn, Dvalinn, Duneyrr and Duraþrór, feed on the tree. The World Tree replenishes itself continually. From its top branches, an eagle perches and controls the wind. At

Yggdrasil's base lays the great dragon or great serpent, known as Niðhǫggr. It chews upon the tree's roots. A squirrel by the name of Ratatoskr runs up and down the trunk, relaying insults between the eagle and the dragon.

Viking mythology was passed down orally, with very little written material available prior to the Eddas of the 13th century. Before the recording of Snorri Sturluson's Prose Edda, it was believed that the nine realms were broken down as follows.

- Asgard: Realm of the Æsir
- Alfheim: Realm of the Bright Elves
- Jotunheim: Realm of the Giants
- Midgard: Realm of the Humans
- Muspelheim: Realm of Fire and Chaos
- Nidavellir: Realm of the Dwarves
- Niflheim: Realm of Ice and Mist
- Svartalfheim: Realm of the Black Elves
- Vanaheim: Realm of the Vanir

Snorri, whose Christianity influenced much of his work, erroneously called dark elves dwarves and thus combined Nidavellir and Svartalfheim. He then added a new realm called Hel that echoed the sentiment of Hell in Christianity.

Since then, Hel has been accepted as being part of one of the Nine Realms of Norse mythology.

Not much description of these worlds exists. What we know has been gathered from references in poems and other medieval texts. Realms beyond Midgard have inspired intrigue with their elusiveness.

Asgard

Asgard is the home of the Æsir. A celestial city, it contains Odin's hall of the dead, Valhalla, and his throne, Hildskjalf, from which he gazes out at the world. Odin rules Asgard with his wife, Frigg. It is also the home of Folkvangr, Freyja's hall of the dead.

Originally Asgard was thought to form a part of Midgard; however, Snorri claims it to be a distinct world connected to the human realm by the Bifrost, or the Rainbow Bridge.

Alfheim

Alfheim, sometimes called *Álfheimr* or *Ljósálfheimr*, is another celestial realm and is home to the light elves. Known as the realm of light, this land is said to be beautiful beyond comprehension, filled with music, art and creativity. Alfheim is described as being next to Asgard. This proximity seems logical, given that the light elves were perhaps similar to minor gods, being depicted as beautiful guardian angels.

Jotunheim

Jotunheim, sometimes called *Jötunheimr*, is the realm of the Jötnar, the sworn enemies of the Æsir, often referred to as giants. Also located alongside Asgard, Jotunheim is known for its lack of order. It is a primordial place where chaos and magic run unchecked. Interestingly, another name for Jotunheim, *Utgard* or *Utangard*, translates as "outside the enclosure." The Norse thought of Midgard and Asgard as being inside a fence, or enclosure of civilization and order and of Jotunheim as being beyond or outside this fence, in the land of chaos.

Jotunheim is separated from Asgard by the river Iving, which never freezes and few dare cross. The terrain here is barren, with dense forests and snowy shores. The giants' main food source is fish obtained from rivers and oceans. No fertile land exists in Jotunheim.

Midgard

Midgard, also called *Miðgarðr* or *Middle Earth*, is the human realm created from the body of the frost giant Ymir. As the name suggests, Midgard is located in the middle of the World Tree, below Asgard. It is connected to Asgard by the Bifrost and surrounded by a huge ocean.

Muspelheim

Muspelheim, also called *Múspellsheimr*, is the primordial realm of fire. It was one of the first realms to come into existence when the great void Ginnungagap spat it out. It is said to be filled with fire and lava, with air so hot it would burn to a crisp whoever breathed it in.

Muspelheim is home to the fire giant, Surtr, fated to rise during Ragnarök to destroy Asgard.

Nidavellir or Svartalfheim

Nidavellir or Svartalfheim (also called *Niðavellir* or *Svartálfaheimr*) is known as the home of the dwarves or dark elves. Situated below Midgard, it is a dark, smoky place, lit only by the light of torches and forges. Nidavellir is known for its craftsmanship and magic. Many powerful objects, like Thor's hammer and Odin's ring, come from this realm.

Niflheim

Niflheim, also written as *Niðavellir*, is the realm of mist and ice. Among the first lands spun into existence along with Muspelheim, it is the root of all life in the cosmos. One of the darkest and most desolate regions, Niflheim contains the "boiling bubbling spring" of Hvergelmir, from which the first giant Ymir forms. It is protected by the great dragon Nidhogg.

Vanaheim

Vanaheim, also known as *Vanaheimr*, is the home of the Vanir. Little description is given of this realm; however, owing to the fertility and magic of its inhabitants, it is assumed to be beautiful and lush, filled with life and abundance.

Helheim

Helheim is the land of the dead, ruled over by Hel, Loki's daughter. Unlike the hell of Christianity, this is not a realm for sinners but merely for any deceased not taken to Valhalla or Folkvangr. Helheim is thought to be a cold and gloomy place where the feeling of happiness may not exist. It is located beneath the roots of the World Tree.

The only way to get to Helheim is by traveling a long, downhill path known as *Helveg* and crossing a river of weapons.

The most populated realm of the dead, the inhabitants here reside in a state of twilight, continuing to live as they might have done on Midgard.

CHAPTER 8

Creatures of Norse Mythology

As with any mythology, Norse lore contains beings and creatures unique to it.

Many contemporary fantasy novels are inspired by Norse beings and creatures. J. R. R. Tolkien's classic *The Lord of the Rings* offers an abundance of Norse-inspired lore, including that of elves, dwarves, trolls and other creatures.

In addition to a variety of general types of beings, the Norse cosmos gives life to a number of notable and famed individual creatures. These diverse entities are explored below.

Groups of Beings

Elves

Two categories of elves were originally distinguished in Norse mythology, the Dökkálfar and the Ljósálfar. The Dökkálfar referred to the dark elves, with skin "blacker than pitch," residing underground. The Ljósálfar signified the light elves, tall, lank demigods with pale skin and hair.

After Snorri's written works of the 13th century, the Dökkálfar became synonymous with the dwarves, and the Ljósálfar came to be known as elves.

The elves were ambivalent when it came to humans; they could choose whether to cause or cure illness, create or remedy misfortune. They tended to stay away from human affairs, unlike the gods.

They were gender fluid and did not subscribe to typical gender roles of society.

Dwarves

Dwarves are known for their wisdom and skill, especially in the areas of magic and forging. Thor's mighty hammer, Mjollnir, and Odin's ring and spear, Draupnir and Gungnir, have been credited to the incredible abilities of the dwarves.

Believed to have evolved from the maggots that sprang from Ymir's rotting corpse during the creation of Midgard, they are thought to be lesser beings by the gods. Although termed "dwarves," they were never described as short. Scholars theorize that the word "lesser" became warped along the way to mean "short."

Sometimes called dark elves or Dökkálfar, dwarves live under the earth. Svartalfheim, the realm of the dwarves, is thought to resemble a complex series of underground labyrinths filled with mines and forges.

Jötnar

The Jötnar (singular Jötunn) are a group of beings residing primarily in the realm of Jotunheim and often in conflict with the gods. The embodiment of chaos, they had powers to rival the Æsir.

Called the giants of Norse mythology, many were the same size as humans, despite their name. Scholars believe that, similar to the case of the dwarves, descriptor words may have been mistranslated. Giants were magical, powerful beings. "Powerful" and "great" could have given the illusion of size, being interpreted as "giant." The Jötnar are also occasionally referred to as "frost giants," perhaps due to their association with the cold realms of Jotunheim and Niflheim, the icy realm which had a part in the birth of Ymir, the first Jötunn.

Trolls

Trolls are a subset of the Jötnar and include two types. One consists of enormous, hideous beasts living in the forests and mountains. The others are small, boulder-like beings residing in caves.

Regardless of the type, they are not depicted as being very intelligent. While not inherently evil, they are self-serving. They have been known to offer favors to travelers.

They also turn to stone in the sunlight. Norse folklore states that lone boulders in fields or atop cliffs were once trolls who turned to stone from staying up too late.

Valkyries

The Valkyries were Disir, a group of female spirits with varied depictions in Norse literature.

They were powerful warriors who rode the battlefields of war, bringing back the slain to Odin in the halls of Valhalla. Beautiful beings, they had hair as bright as the sun or as dark as the black night, and they were highly skilled in war. It is said the Valkyries decided which warriors were killed in battle and which weren't. They were held in high esteem by female Vikings.

Draugar

The Draugar are the Norse version of zombies or the undead.

They were the repossessed remains of Vikings who had died, often those who were thought to be particularly greedy or evil in their living years.

Armed with enhanced strength, they aimed to protect their treasure and graves from being disturbed. They could also torment the living who they felt had wronged them while they were alive.

Able to change their shape and size at will, they could swallow their victims whole. They were thought to be able to faze through solid rock and possess a strong stench of decay.

The Draugar could be killed if their bodies were burnt.

Haugbui

Similar to the Draugar is the Haugbui, an earth-bound soul concerned with protecting their grave goods after death. Unlike the Draugar, these souls cannot leave their locations. They are bound to their gravesites and are generally harmless.

Norns

The Norns are among the most powerful beings in the Nordic cosmos as they control fate, weaving the destinies of humans and gods alike. In the Prose Edda, the Norns are depicted as three female beings called:

- Urðr (or Wyrd): meaning "The Past" as well as simply "Fate"

- Verdandi: meaning "What Is Presently Coming Into Being"

- Skuld: meaning "What Shall Be"

The Norns were credited with fates both wanted and unwanted, good and evil, and their outcomes did not appear to be changeable once set. Some stories tell of the Norns visiting families at the birth of a child to establish the newborn's destiny, including the length and events of its life. The Norns are also responsible for taking care of Yggdrasil, the World Tree, by watering it daily from the Well of Urd.

Individual Creatures

Jörmungandr

Jörmungandr, also known as the Midgard Serpent or the World Serpent, is the son of Loki and the giantess Angrboda. When the gods received the prophecy that the three children of Loki and Angrboda, namely Jörmungandr, Fenrir and Hel, would cause trouble in the future, Odin sought to confine them. Jörmungandr was thrown into the seas of Midgard. He continued growing until he was so large that he circled the whole of Midgard, biting his own tail. Surrounding the earth, the great serpent holds everything in place.

Jörmungandr's enemy is Thor, and they are said to battle at Ragnarök and kill each other. Jörmungandr will release his tail and rise upward, poisoning the skies and oceans with his venom. This is one of the omens to mark the beginning of the end of the world.

Fenrir

Fenrir is the giant black wolf son of Loki and Angrboda, sibling to Jörmungandr and Hel. Fenrir grew so fast and large that he became a threat to the gods. Odin foresaw Fenrir bringing about the end of the world, and the gods plotted to entrap him.

After testing two separate chains of their own which could not hold the powerful wolf, the Æsir sent a messenger to the dwarves for assistance. In order to fashion a unique, unbreakable chain, the dwarves made use of six mystical or inconceivable elements: the sound of a cat's footfalls, the beard of a woman, the roots of a mountain, the sinews of a bear, the breath of a fish and the spit of a bird. Their skill resulted in a deceptively soft, ribbon-like chain which they termed Gleipnir.

Though the gods encouraged Fenrir to again test his might, he felt apprehension in approaching the unusual binding and would only proceed if one of the gods volunteered to place a hand in his mouth, in good faith.

Tyr, the god of justice and treaties, was the only one willing to step forward for the task. The giant wolf was indeed unable to break free of Gleipnir and bit off Tyr's hand in his rage.

Fenrir is fated at Ragnarök to break out of his bindings and wreak havoc on Midgard before devouring Odin. He, in turn, is slain by Odin's son, Vidar.

Sleipnir

Sleipnir is the powerful eight-legged horse ridden by Odin. Swift and intuitive, he could carry a rider anywhere in the nine realms, finding the fastest and safest routes available. His name, meaning "the sliding one," recalls his skill in slipping easily between worlds, including the realm of the dead.

Sleipnir's magical origin is relayed in the *Prose Edda*. After the construction of the nine realms, the gods prepared to build a protective wall around Asgard and Valhalla. A being stepped forward to offer his labor in exchange for Freya's hand in marriage, as well as the sun and the moon. Disinclined to part with such rewards, the gods struck a deal in which the builder had to complete the wall by the following winter using only the help of his horse, Svaðilfari. It soon became apparent that the horse was a mighty and fast worker, and the work would be finished on time. The gods commanded Loki to delay the process. He transformed himself into a mare to lure the stallion away from his duties, and the wall was left incomplete. Svaðilfari eventually caught and mated with Loki, resulting in the magical eight-legged offspring, Sleipnir. The new horse was claimed by Odin to be his personal steed.

Tanngnjóstr and Tanngrisnir

Tanngnjóstr and Tanngrisnir ("teeth-grinder" and "teeth-barer") were two magical goats that pulled Thor's chariot. The sound of thunder and the flash of sparks and lightning would set off as the chariot moved forth and traveled across the skies. The goats occasionally provided a food source for Thor and others. They could be brought back to life by reassembling their bones and skin. Thor frequently killed and ate them when he was hungry, only to revive them again at a later stage.

Huginn and Muninn

Huginn (which translates to "thought") and Muninn ("mind") were Odin's ravens. They were his eyes and ears on Midgard. They would relay all they had seen to him and could often be found perched on his shoulders, whispering into Odin's ears.

Some sagas suggest that Odin was often more interested in Huginn and Muninn than in his own court. The ravens may have been a metaphor for Odin casting his thoughts over the lands in a meditative state, and he is said to have feared sometimes that they might not return. Ravens are depicted with Odin on many Norse artifacts.

Ratatoskr

Ratatoskr is a squirrel that runs up and down the World Tree, Yggdrasil. He conveys messages between the eagle perched in the upper branches, Veðrfölnir, and the dragon at the roots, Níðhöggr. He liked to stir up trouble between the two by adding insults to the messages. In some accounts, his craftiness is taken further into provoking the eagle and the dragon into attacking the tree, contributing to a cycle of destruction and regrowth.

Nidhogg

Nidhogg, or Níðhöggr, is the dragon that lays at the roots of Yggdrasil, the World Tree and is also seen as the protector of the spring Hvergelmir in Niflheim. Called the Great Serpent, he continually chews upon the roots of the World Tree. With a scaled, serpentine body, he possesses huge, bat-like wings and horns atop his head.

In one poem, Nidhogg is described as ruling over Nastrond, a dark realm reserved for the most dishonorable departed, such as oath-breakers, adulterers and murderers. Sent down into Nastrond at their passing, they await being consumed by this great beast.

CHAPTER 9

Odds and Ends

Death and the Afterlife

The Vikings had specific traditions and rituals surrounding death based on their belief in and views of the afterlife. Exploring Valhalla and beyond, this section will take you through everything related to the dead: funeral rites, rebirth and the various realms of the afterlife.

The Viking Funeral

Viking funerals were social and familial affairs.

Burials were handled similarly to Egyptian burials, the dead buried with artifacts and riches. Elaborate rituals and traditions accompanied death and funerals.

There were two ways to reach the afterlife: cremation or burial.

During the Pagan era of the Viking Age, the deceased were cremated on a funeral pyre. The Norse believed the smoke from the fire would help ferry the dead into the afterlife. The funeral pyre was set alight and burned so hot it turned everything—even bone—to ash. The ashes were collected and placed in an urn to be buried in the funeral mound.

As Christianity gained influence, fewer and fewer cremations were seen, Viking families opting instead to place the deceased whole in the burial mound.

Graves varied greatly from shallow, haphazard sites for slaves to elaborate mounds dedicated to multiple individuals.

Burial mounds were often shaped to look like overturned ships or, in the cases of the very wealthy, contained actual ships buried with the deceased.

Funeral sites contained everything the departed would require in the afterlife. These items would be anything important to or representative of the deceased. Families would take turns placing these "grave goods" inside the grave before it was covered up.

The size and fullness of the graves correlated to the individual's wealth and status within the community. Archaeologists have been able to determine what kind of person was buried in a particular site based on items found with the dead. A merchant woman might be buried with merchant scrolls, money, a horse, craft items, jewelry or keys. A warrior man might be accompanied by weapons, shields, heirlooms or slaves.

The dead were buried in new clothes specifically prepared for the ceremony. Formalities were accompanied by songs of mourning, chants, food and alcohol. People gathered and told tales of the departed.

The only people not a part of these rituals were slaves, who were often buried in shallow, unmarked graves, if they died before their masters.

Ghost Prevention

An interesting aspect of Norse views surrounding death is that they had a strong belief in ghosts. They took special precautions when handling the dead to ensure they would not be haunted or tormented by the ghosts of their ancestors.

These precautions might include:

- Wrapping the head of a corpse, so it could not see where it was being taken and find its way home again.

- Carrying the body out of a home feet-first, again so the spirit would not be able to see where it was headed.

- Sewing the toes or the feet together to stop reanimated corpses from walking out of their graves. Vikings could occasionally break the legs of the deceased as well.

- Only answering a door to three knocks. It was believed that spirits knocked only once and that, should you answer the door for a spirit, you would likely never be heard from again.

- Using talismans and protective symbolism in the funeral process.

- Creating a "corpse door," one of the more labor-intensive yet trusted ways of avoiding a haunting if the deceased died indoors. A house could be fitted with a door that was solely used to remove the dead and was then bricked up again. It was believed that spirits could only enter through a door they had left through.

Rebirth

Rebirth is an important concept to Vikings, strongly tied to the connection they felt with their ancestors. They believed that the souls of their ancestors could be reborn into their families. Many Viking children were named after the deceased to invoke the spirit of those who came before.

The concept of rebirth is also portrayed in the story of Ragnarök. Thought to be influenced by Christianity, Snorri's version of the End of Worlds features rebirth as a principal theme.

Reward and Punishment of Life Deeds

Unlike many religions, Viking traditions, for the most part, did not demonstrate a concept of punishment and reward in relation to death. The state of your afterlife was not dependent on what kind of person you were but rather unfolded through happenstance and luck.

While Norse mythology does contain a Hel, it contrasts with the hell described in Christianity. Vikings believed Helheim to simply be the realm where the dead lived rather than where they might pay penance for their deeds. The lifestyle of the living had little weight on the state of their afterlife.

The description of Nastrond in the Norse poem, the Völuspá, is perhaps the only reference to a place of punishment upon death, and it is estimated to be heavily influenced by Christian beliefs. As stated earlier, Nastrond (meaning "shore of corpses") represented an underground realm at the feet of Nidhogg, the dragon. Wayward souls such as adulterers, oath-breakers and murderers were sent there and awaited their turn to be chewed upon by the Great Serpent.

Parts of the Self

Norse mythology recognizes four distinct parts of human individuals:

- Hamr: the physical appearance

- Hugr: the character or personality

- Fylgja: the spirit animal or familiar

- Hamingja: the quality of life

At the time of death, all four parts of the self can go to a single location, or they can be split up. There have been cases where a person's Hugr, or personality, was said to pass into the body of a newborn while their Fylgja, or spirit animal, remained in Hel.

There was no judgment or rule about where each of these parts went. The soul was free to choose where possible. Otherwise, it was down to luck.

Hamr

The Hamr is one's physical appearance, their visible form. The appearance could, at times, be manipulated to change, the process behind the idea of shapeshifting, manipulating one's Hamr.

Hugr

The Hugr represented one's character and personality. It is believed that the Hugr is never destroyed but merely moves to another plane of existence, waiting to be reborn.

Draugar were creatures that came into existence when the Hugr of a greedy or evil person did not move on to the afterlife and decided to reinhabit the body and wreak havoc on the human world.

Fylgja

The Fylgja denoted the person's spirit animal. As unique to the individual as their Hugr, it aligned with their personality traits. For example, a fierce warrior might have a wolf as their Fylgja, while a shy person could have a rabbit.

Hamingja

Hamingja is the quality of life you share with your family. It is said to remain behind after the rest of the soul has departed the human realm.

In this way, a person's bad luck or curses, or their good luck and prosperity, could remain with their family long after they had died.

Realms of the Afterlife

Vikings, like many other cultures, believed in the afterlife. However, just as their religious base was polytheistic, the Norse afterlife also contained a multitude of paths.

Vikings saw death not as an end but as the beginning of a new life to be spent with the gods. This belief influenced how funeral rites were performed and who the Vikings prayed to for protection, as well as where they believed they went in the end.

The choice of destination was not made by the individual but rather by the gods in charge of the various realms. Vikings were selected by the gods themselves, or the messengers of the gods, to be sent to a specific afterlife.

Valhalla

Valhalla, or "Hall of the Fallen," is perhaps the most well-known afterlife, as well as the most sought-after during the Viking Age. It is presided over by Odin and his Valkyries.

As the realm reserved for heroes of war, only the best warriors could hope to end up in this paradise. Warriors who died in battle could be chosen by the Valkyries to live the rest of their days in Odin's hall until called upon to fight with the Æsir gods at Rangnarök.

Until then, these warriors are invited to dine, drink, fight, heal and tell stories in the hall of the Allfather and the other Æsir gods.

However, not every fallen hero was taken to Valhalla. Those slain in battle were assumed to have a 50% chance of ending up in Fólkvangr, Freya's hall of the dead.

Fólkvangr

Fólkvangr, known as the "field of the people," was the realm of the dead overseen by Freya, the goddess of lust, fertility and beauty. She collects the other half of warriors who die on battlefields.

Not much exists by way of Fólkvangr's description; however, we can infer that it was a beautiful and abundant place, corresponding to Freya's personality and characteristics.

Helheim

Helheim could be considered the most highly populated afterlife realm. Ruled over by Hel, Loki's daughter, it is believed impossible to escape from unless Hel herself grants permission to leave. Apart from the Æsir attempt to have Baldr released, not many others have tried to leave Hel.

People who died of illness or old age were sent to Helheim. Those who did not die in battle would sometimes cut themselves or crush their bones on their deathbeds to trick Hel into thinking they had died a violent, noble death and sending them to a more glamorous afterlife.

Helheim is located under Midgard and can only be accessed by the Helvegr, the Road to Hell, or by crossing the Uncrossable River. The gates of Helheim are guarded by a great dog. Scholars debate whether this is the wolf Fenrir, Hel's brother. Helheim is described as dark, foggy and gloomy.

Unlike Hell in Christianity, where only the wicked are sent for punishment, Helheim is merely the land of the dead. The only entrance requirement is death. The souls in Helheim live out their lives in the same manner as when they were alive. They eat, drink, hunt, fight and craft as they always had—all while waiting for Ragnarök.

Helheim is thus the default locale for the afterlife. Sagas tell tales of families being reunited in Helheim after death and continuing their lives together there.

Nastrond

As discussed earlier, Nastrond was an afterlife realm that may or may not have been a part of pre-Christian Norse beliefs. If it was a realm upheld in the Viking Age, however, it would have been one to be feared.

As the destination for evil or socially unacceptable souls, Nastrond delivered retribution for earthly crimes. Being sent to the "Corpse Shore" meant traveling to a lower level of Helheim. Here, at the feet of Nidhogg, the dragon, poison dripped from the ceiling, and snakes writhed on the floor. Busy chewing upon the roots of Yggdrasil, the World Tree, Nidhogg would then chew upon the corpses that found their way here.

The Realm of Ran

Considering how much time the Vikings spent on the water, it is no wonder they had a patron sea god to watch over them and their deaths at sea.

Ran was a giantess who claimed the ocean floor as her domain. Hers was said to be the shiniest and richest of the afterlives. All the treasure that sank into the sea made its way to her realm for her enjoyment.

Sailors who died at sea were welcomed to the realm of Ran. Some myths claim that Ran herself would capture sailors in her nets and drag them under so that she may have company in her halls.

Ragnarök

Just as Norse mythology accepted death as an inevitable part of human experience, so too did it contain ideas about the mortality of the gods. While long-lived and powerful, the Norse gods were not seen as invincible.

Since the creation of the World Tree in the early days of the Norse cosmos, the Norns, in their spinning of fates at the tree's roots, had foretold the coming of Ragnarök. Meaning "fate of the gods" or "twilight of the gods," Ragnarök equated to a clashing together of the forces of order and chaos and the destruction of the world as it was known to be. The gods' might would be tested, and many would perish as all manner of god, creature and being entered into conflict.

There is some contention surrounding Ragnarök as scholars debate its origins. Two versions of Ragnarök exist. In one, everything is destroyed, and all life ceases to be. The world is returned to Ginnungagap, the vast void. The second version contains a rebirth of creation in which a few gods and two humans survive to repopulate the earth.

While it is believed that the story of rebirth may be evidence of Christian influence on the mythology of old, it is difficult to access for certain the original picture of Ragnarök. The elements featuring renewal are included below for consideration and are also widely employed today in various retellings. It can be useful, however, to bear in mind the possibility that they may not have been included in the initial Ragnarök account.

Beginning of Ragnarök

The murder of Baldr was seen as an event signifying the beginning of Ragnarök. The Vikings thus believed Ragnarök was happening in their time. They felt it was already the end of days and that the end of the world was in their near future.

It was prophesied that Ragnarök would begin with three cruel winters and the abandonment of principles. The sky would darken as the sun was devoured and the stars vanished. The dead would rise to fight at the side of their patron gods. Creatures would emerge from the depths and shadows to wreak havoc and chaos. Baldr was foretold to finally return to Asgard.

Fenrir is said to break his bonds and run about Midgard, destroying all in his path. Jörmungandr releases his tail, rising from the seas to poison the sky and oceans with his venom. Hel will raise her army of the dead, which she then gives to Loki to lead in battle against the Æsir gods, who bound him to the rock to be poisoned by Skadi for all eternity.

Surtr, the fire giant, rises again.

The Battle

Loki arrives at Asgard's gate with his army of the dead and the fire giant Surtr as well as other giants and dark forces. It is said that he will arrive on the ship Naglfar, an underworld boat built from the fingernails of the dead.

Surtr wields a massive sword wreathed in flame, brighter than the sun. The forces arrive at Vigrid, the official battlefield of Ragnarök, and are met by Odin and other gods and warrior forces from Valhalla and, possibly, Fólkvangr.

Who Is Fated to Die in Ragnarök?

The gods, up to this point, may have appeared immortal and youthful. They have, in fact, kept young and strong with some assistance. Idunn, the goddess of youth, spring and rejuvenation, offers apples of immortality, from which the gods continually benefit. But should they stop eating them, or should they be felled in battle, they can die, as is seen with Baldr and other gods.

As the forces of chaos and order clash at Ragnarök, Odin is killed by Fenrir, the great black wolf and son of Loki and Angrboda. Fenrir is, in turn, brought down by Odin's son, Vidar.

Thor and Jörmungandr battle, resulting in each of them killing the other. Thor, after slaying the great sea serpent, manages to walk nine steps before falling to Jörmungandr's venom.

The fight between Loki and Heimdall results in a mutual death.

Freyr, brother to Freya and son of Njord, is slain by Surtr before the fire giant sets all of Asgard ablaze.

And so Asgard falls, burned to the ground.

Who Will Survive?

Only a few gods survive the aftermath of Ragnarök. These include Odin's wife Frigg, his sons Vidar and Baldr, Thor's wife Sif, the Vanir goddess Freya, the goddess of rejuvenation Idunn, and the underworld goddess, Loki's daughter Hel.

Helheim can now be entered and left as one pleases, suggesting that Hel somehow lost her powers during the final battle.

There are no foretold survivors of giants or other creatures.

According to one poem, two humans, Lif and Lifthrasir ("Life" and "Vitality"), will survive the battle and go on to repopulate Midgard.

What Comes After Ragnarök?

When the Æsir return to Asgard, in the ash where the city once stood, they find gold game pieces they used to play with and feel nostalgic. They begin telling tales of the past and setting the stage for the future.

The battlefields on the plains of Ithavoll will spur the creation of Gimlé, a hall rumored to be more beautiful than sunlight, that would become the new home of the gods.

CHAPTER 10

Norse Mythology in Today's World

Even after more than eight centuries, we are still finding interest in Norse mythology around the globe today.

While the digital age has provided exposure to modern trends around the world, it has also been an avenue for the exploration of ancient culture.

From movies to books, music, fashion and beyond, aspects of life continue to unfold that show influence from ancient mythologies. While Greek mythology has had a strong foothold in popular culture for quite some time, Norse lore is expanding its presence globally. Below are a few of the modern avenues Norse myth and Viking culture have taken.

Movies and Television

The History Channel's *Vikings* series, based on the sagas of Ragnar Lothbrok, is some of the best-known Norse content in the media. Depicting the life of Ragnar as he rises from a farmer to a Scandinavian king, the series also follows the conquests of his sons in their raids of England and the Mediterranean. This historical drama aims to be true to the sagas and culture of the Vikings while also taking some liberty for storytelling purposes.

Norsemen is a Norwegian comedy series that parodies Viking culture in the village of Norheim in the year 790. It follows various characters as they handle day-to-day life and conflicts with a healthy dose of occasionally dark humor. The series was filmed in Norway in both Norwegian and English, each scene being filmed twice, and met with positive reception in both Norway and abroad.

DreamWorks' animated 2010 film, *How to Train Your Dragon*, along with its sequels and mini-series, was based on the book by Cressida Cowell and created for kids, but appeals to a broader audience as well. Lightly referencing elements of Norse mythology and history, it also includes a number of Viking stereotypes. It is, nonetheless, a fun story meant for entertainment and could be a starting point for deeper investigation of Norse themes.

And, of course, the Thor and Loki of Marvel comics, first popularized in the 1960s, have made their way into Disney's Marvel Cinematic Universe in the form of three Thor movies, a Loki mini-series and several Avenger films. In this universe prominently featuring the gods of thunder and mischief,

Loki is cast as the half-brother of Thor and is seen as his antithesis, impeding his plans at each turn.

Games

Video games have seen a huge rise in Norse content as they offer a visual and interactive way to experience Viking Age history and mythology. Ubisoft's popular *Assassin's Creed Valhalla* follows Viking raider Eivor Varinsdottir as she attempts to establish a new Viking clan in the heart of England.

The dark fantasy action-adventure game *Hellblade: Senua's Sacrifice* has won international awards for gameplay and story. Set in the Viking Age, it involves Celtic warrior Senua as she faces Helheim to rescue her dead lover.

The recent Norse-era installments of the *God of War* series have been well received, with the 2018 release achieving Game of the Year recognitions. 2022's *God of War Ragnarök* is the much-anticipated finale to the Norse theme.

Music

There has been an emergence in the last thirty years or so of a music genre called Viking metal or Pagan metal. With lyrics and themes based on Norse mythology, it features many Pagan motifs.

Artists have sprung up all around Scandinavia and broader northern European regions. Ensiferum from Finland and Heidevolk from the Netherlands are two folk metal bands with several albums out. Týr, from the Norse god of war and justice, hails from the Faroe Islands and centers its lyrics on Norse mythology and history, as does Amon Amarth from Sweden.

Books

English author J. R. R. Tolkien drew heavily on inspiration from Norse beings and creatures in his classic works *The Hobbit* and *The Lord of the Rings*. These novels paved the way for others in the high-fantasy genre as dwarves, elves and giants became staples of fantasy fiction.

Neil Gaiman's 2001 award-winning novel *American Gods* changed how many approached using theology in their writing. Pitting the gods of modern culture against those of various ancient mythologies, the story's success later propelled it to a tv-series adaptation. More significantly, in 2017 Gaiman published a retelling of the tales of the Norse gods in his popular work entitled *Norse Mythology*.

As previously mentioned, the Thor of Marvel comics began his journey in 1962. Under the creation of Stan Lee, Larry Lieber and Jack Kirby, the hero arose in the second wave of comic popularity, known as the Silver Age of comics. Thor was inspired by the desire for a character with more than human strength and with the unique appeal of Norse origins. He evolved over the years to become one of the most popular superheroes and Avengers.

American author Rick Riordan, after exploring the Greek mythology world in his comedic Percy Jackson series for young readers, spun into Norse roots from the same universe with his Magnus Chase novels. Combining ancient Norse characters with modern-day teenage families, his stories have sparked mass interest and appeal with a global audience.

Of course, not all media depictions are correct. But these are not documentaries and textbooks; they are interpretations and retellings of the tales of old, often through the filter of how they might relate to us today.

Norse history and myth may never stop being a catalyst for inspiration. Without the Norns to guide us, it is impossible to predict which road the stories will take us down next. But we can presume that Norse mythology will remain relevant for years to come.

Conclusion

Taking a dive into the world of Viking life and Norse mythology reveals how complex Scandinavian history can be.

We have just scratched the surface of the Norse cosmos. Scholars are still coming up with new ideas and interpretations of texts that are nearly a millennium old.

Numerous aspects of Viking society were covered in the previous chapters, from famous warriors to the structure of their daily lives. Norse art, architecture and runes expand the picture of Viking life. The introduction of gods, creatures and realms, along with a number of their stories help illustrate the Viking worldview. And finally, the accounts of the end times demonstrate the Viking outlook on the potential outcomes of the human race and their way of life.

It is hoped that these explorations can inspire further readings of Norse mythology.

The Poetic and Prose Eddas offer a rich collection of stories and a deeper look into medieval Norse life. There are fantastic translations available online for free. These artful verses provide a compelling picture of Norse mythology from an era much closer to, if not quite in, the Viking Age.

If you enjoyed this book, please leave a review. Your comments are much appreciated!

Stay tuned for more mythology coming soon.

Glossary

Æsir: [pronounced *ICE-ear*] the main Norse gods, the gods of order, residing in Asgard

Alfheim: [pronounced *ALF-hame*] realm of the Bright Elves

Allfather: another name for Odin

Anglo-Saxon: describing people who inhabited England and Wales during the Middle Ages

Art of Seidr: magic pertaining to the shaping of the future

Asgard: [pronounced *As-guard*] Realm of the Æsir

Ask: the first woman, carved from an ash branch and brought to life by Odin and his brothers, Ve and Vili

Audhumbla: [pronounced *Ow-doom-lar*] the sacred cow who fed Ymir, the first of the Jötnar, and freed Buri, the first of the Æsir, during the creation of the Norse universe

Austri: the dwarf who holds up the sky in the east

Baldr: [pronounced *Bal-durr*] god of light, peace, and beauty; son of Odin; brother to Hodr

Bergelmir: [pronounced *Berg-ell-mere*] the only giant male to survive the battle with the gods, along with his wife, during the creation of the Norse cosmos

Berserkers: (translates to "Bear-skin") highly skilled warriors who fought in a trance-induced state of frenzy and rage

Bestla: [pronounced *Bes-tla*] wife of Bor

Bifrost: [pronounced *BYE-frost or BEE-frost*] (translates to "The Rainbow Bridge") the bridge between Midgard and Asgard

Bor: son of Buri

Brud hlaup: a footrace between in-laws following the wedding ceremony to determine which family would serve the wine at the reception

Buri: the first god who was licked out of the ice by Audhumbla; father of Bor; grandfather of Odin

Carvel ships: ships with strong, heavy frames to which planks of any quality wood were attached to build the hull

Clinker ship: ships with overlapping, riveted planks that were shaped by a lightweight frame and keel

Dökkálfar: (translates to "dark elves") demi-gods of dark skin who live underground; synonymous with dwarves

Draugar: reanimated corpses of the recently dead

Draupnir: Odin's ring

Dwarves: (sing. Dwarf) (sometimes called "Dökkálfar") residents of Svartalfheim; underground dwellers; skilled smiths

Elves: (also known as "Ljósálfar") residents of Alfheim; entities of light and grace; demi-gods

Embla: [pronounced *Em-bler*] The first male, carved from an elm branch by Odin and his brothers, Ve and Vili

Etiological myth: a myth that describes the origin of something

Fenrir: [pronounced *FEN-rear*] black wolf son of Loki, fated to slay Odin during Ragnarok

Fólkvangr: a realm of the afterlife; the hall of Freya

Freki: one of Odin's wolf familiars, along with Geri, who accompanied him onto battlefields to eat the corpses of his enemies

Freya: [pronounced *FREY-yaa*] goddess of lust, fertility, and beauty; daughter of Njord; sister to Freyr

Freyr: [pronounced *FREY-ur*] god of harvest, wealth, and virility; brother to Freya; son of Njord

Frigg: the wife of Odin; goddess of love and marriage

Fylgja: the spirit totem of the soul

Geri: one of Odin's wolf familiars, along with Freki, who accompanied him onto battlefields to eat the corpses of his enemies

Gimlé: Hall of Sunlight; new Asgard

Ginnungagap: The vast empty blackness that predates existence

Gjallarhorn: the horn blown by Heimdall to signal the beginning of Ragnarök

Gullveig: [pronounced *Gool-vague*] (translates to "gold-greed") referring to Freya, crediting her with causing the Æsir-Vanir war

Gungnir: Odin's spear

Gylfaginning: (translates to "the Tricking of Gylfi") A manuscript forming part of the Prose Edda, written by Snorri Sturluson, containing questions and answers on specific aspects of Norse mythology

Hamingja: quality of life of the soul

Hamr: the physical appearance or the soul

Hangrok: a harness dress held up by leather straps and brooches

Haugbui: earth-bound spirits

Heiðr: Freya in disguise when she traveled to Asgard as a practitioner of *seidr*

Heimdall: [pronounced *HAME-doll*] watchman of the Æsir gods; keeper of the Bifrost

Hel: goddess of death; daughter of the Jötnar Loki and Angrboda; Queen of Helheim

Helheim: the realm of Hel; the underworld

Helveg: the road to Hel

Hildisvíni: Freya's battle-boar who is suspected of being her lover in disguise

Himinbjörg: home of Heimdall located at the foot of the Bifrost

Hlidskjalf: Odin's throne that allows him to see into all nine realms when he sits on it

Hodr: god of darkness; son of Odin; brother of Baldr

Höttr: hood-like head covering with a hole for the face

Huginn: (translates to "thought") one of Odin's two ravens, along with Muninn ("mind"), that reported to him about the goings-on of Midgard and the nine realms

Hugr: the character portion of the soul

Hvergelmir: the spring that feeds the waters below the World Tree

Idunn: [pronounced *I-dunn* or *I-thoon*] goddess of youth and spring

Jarl: the Noble class of Viking society

Járngreipr: (translates to "iron grippers") the gloves worn by Thor, made by the dwarves

Jörmungandr: [pronounced *YOUR-moon-gand-er*] (also called "The Great Serpent") the serpentine son of Loki who was thrown into the seas of Midgard by Odin

Jotunheim: [pronounced *YO-tun-hame*] realm of the giants and chaos

Jötnar: (sing. Jötunn) being of chaos, often referred to as giants, inhabitants of Jotunheim, often in conflict with the gods

Karl: the working class of Viking society; "freeman"

Kirtle: long linen undershirt that often fell to the knees

Knörr: Viking merchant ship

Knotwork: art technique composed of intertwining and weaving patterns

Kohl: black powder worn on the eye

Langskip: Viking warship

Laugardagur: (also called Lördag) Saturday; the day of bathing

Ljósálfar: (translates to "light elves") demi-gods who live in Alfheim

Loki: [pronounced *LOW-key* or *LOCK-ee*] god of deception and trickery; Jötunn half-brother of Odin; father to Hel, Fenrir, and Jörmungandr; mother to Sleipnir

Longhouse: typical house design of the Viking Age; inverted ship-shaped houses measuring up to 72 feet long (22 meters) and 16 feet wide (5 meters)

Mani: [pronounced *MAH-nee*] the divinity of the moon

Megingjörd: the belt worn by Thor to double his strength

Midgard: [pronounced *Midd-gard* or *Mith-gard*] (also called Miðgarðr or Middle Earth) Realm of the Humans

Mimir: [pronounced *MEE-mere*] a water spirit; wisest of the Æsir gods; beheaded during the Æsir-Vanir war

Mímisbrunnr: one of two wells, along with Urðarbrunnr, residing at the base of the world tree, Yggdrasil

Mjollnir: [pronounced *MIOL-near*] Thor's war hammer fashioned by the dwarves

Muninn: (translates to "mind") one of Odin's two ravens, along with Huginn ("thought"), that reported to him about the goings-on of Midgard and the nine realms

Muspelheim: [pronounced *Moo-spell-hame*] (Múspellsheimr) Realm of Fire and chaos

Mythology: a collection of stories pertaining to the understanding of a people

Nidavellir: [pronounced *Nith-a-vell-ear*] Realm of the Dwarves

Nidhogg: [pronounced *Nee-thog*] (also called *Niðhǫggr* or "The Great Serpent") the dragon that chews on the roots of Yggdrasil; ruler over Nastrond, the realm of the damned

Niflheim: [pronounced *Niff-el-hame*] realm of ice and mist

Njord: [pronounced *Nigh-ord*] god of the wind and sea; father to Freyr and Freya

Nóatún: (translates to "Place of Ships") the home of Njord

Nordi: the dwarf who holds up the sky in the north

Norns: three female entities who control the fates of everyone in the universe

Norse: Scandinavian people and culture, especially in medieval times

Odin: [pronounced *Oh-deen* or *Oh-thin*] King of Asgard; ruler of the Æsir; god of wisdom and war

Odr: husband of Freya

Pagan: term for people in the Middle Ages who practiced polytheistic or ethnic religions, non-Christian

Paganism: following the practices of worshiping many gods

Pluralism: the act of acknowledging or adhering to two or more religions at the same time

Poetic Edda: (also known as the "elder Edda") Norse collection of poems, written down in Iceland in the 13th century, containing skaldic oral poetry of previous centuries

Polytheistic: relating to the worship of multiple gods

Prose Edda: (also known as the "Younger Edda") Norse manuscript written in Iceland by 13th-century historian, Snorri Sturluson, to preserve the poetic style of Viking-era skalds

Puttee: fabric leg wrappings; strips of dense fabric wound around the lower legs to keep them warm and dry

Ragnarök: [pronounced *RAG-nar-rock*] the final battle between chaos and order leading to the destruction (and potential rebirth) of the world; the reckoning of the gods

Ran: giantess who dwells on the ocean floor; ruler of the realm of Ran, destined for seafarers who died at sea

Ratatoskr: [pronounced *Rat-at-osk*] the squirrel that runs up and down the World Tree conveying messages back and forth between the eagle residing in its branches and the dragon laying at its roots

Runes: Norse writing system, alphabet

Scandinavia: sub-region of northern Europe generally including the countries of Norway, Sweden and Denmark, and occasionally Iceland and the Faroe Islands

Shield-maidens: female warrior Vikings

Skadi: the Jötunn goddess of winter who suspended the poisonous serpent above Loki in his punishment for aiding in the death of the god Baldr; married to Njord for a time

Skaldic poetry: an oral form of poetry originating in Norway and developed by Icelandic poets, or skalds, between the 9th and 13th centuries

Sleipnir: [pronounced *Sleyp-near*] Odin's eight-legged horse; son of Loki

Sol: [pronounced *soul*] the divinity of the sun

Sundri: the dwarf who holds up the sky in the south

Surtr: Fire giant residing in Muspelheim; is said to burn Asgard to the ground during Ragnarök

Svartalfheim: realm of the Black Elves and Dwarves

Tallow: rendered beef or mutton fat

Tanngnjóstr, Tanngrisnir: magical rams that pulled Thor's chariot; were frequently eaten by Thor and reanimated

Thökk: the giantess, thought to be Loki in disguise, who refused to weep for the death of Baldr, thereby foiling the Æsir's attempt to rescue Baldr from Helheim

Thor: god of thunder; son of Odin

Thrall: the slave class of Viking society

Trelleborg: Viking stronghold structure

Trolls: subset of giants with limited intelligence

Tyr: [pronounced *Tire or Tee-ya*] one-armed god of justice

Urðarbrunnr: (also known as "Fate's Well") the well used to water the roots of the World Tree, Yggdrasil

Valhalla: Odin's hall of the dead

Vali: son of Odin; avenger of Baldr's death

Valkyries: [pronounced *Vall-KI-ree* or *Varl-KOO-ree*] minor deities in service of Odin; female warriors who brought slain warriors to Valhalla on behalf of Odin

Vanaheim: [pronounced *Varna-heim*] realm of the Vanir gods

Vanir: [pronounced *Var-near*] minor gods of Vanaheim

Varangian Guard: (also called the "Emperor's Wineskins") an elite fighting force and bodyguards to the Byzantine Emperors and their families

Vatni ausinn: naming ceremony for babies, held nine days after birth

Ve: [pronounced *Vay*] god of creation; Odin's brother; gifted movement and intelligence to Ask and Embla

Vestri: the dwarf who holds up the sky in the west

Vidar: the silent god of vengeance; second strongest god after Thor; brother of Thor, son of Odin, one of the few gods to survive Ragnarök

Viking Age: c 790–1100 AD

Viking: a term used to describe warriors and other settlers of Scandinavian descent who raided through the Viking Age

Vili: [pronounced *Vee-lee*] god of creation; Odin's brother; gifted shape, speech, feelings and five senses to the humans Ask and Embla.

Völuspa: (translates to "The Seeress' Prophecy") a poem of creation from the Poetic Edda

Yggdrasil: [pronounced *EEG-drass-ill*] (translates as "The World Tree") an eternal green ash tree linking the nine realms together

Ymir: [pronounced *EE-mear*] the first being of the universe; the giant whose body was used to create the world

Zoomorphism: the art of depicting gods or humans as non-human entities such as animals and beasts

References

"15 Scariest Norse Mythology Creatures [Monster List]." *Norse and Viking Mythology [Best Blog] - Vkngjewelry*, Jan. 21, 2019, blog.vkngjewelry.com/en/creatures-of-norse-mythology/.

"15 Unique Creatures of Norse Mythology." *Symbol Sage*, Jan. 28, 2021, symbolsage.com/norse-mythology-creatures-list/.

"Aesir - New World Encyclopedia." *Www.newworldencyclopedia.org*, www.newworldencyclopedia.org/entry/Aesir.

"An Overview of Architecture in the Viking Age." *RTF | Rethinking the Future*, Nov. 16, 2021, www.re-thinkingthefuture.com/architectural-community/a5886-an-overview-of-architecture-in-the-viking-age/.

Apel, Thomas. "Thor." *Mythopedia*, Nov. 14, 2021, mythopedia.com/topics/thor.

"Appearance - National Museum of Denmark." *National Museum of Denmark*, 2019, en.natmus.dk/historical-knowledge/denmark/prehistoric-period-until-1050-ad/the-viking-age/the-people/appearance/.

"Art of the Viking Age – Smarthistory." *Smarthistory.org*, smarthistory.org/viking-art/.

"Ásgard and the Nine Worlds of Norse Mythology." *Sky HISTORY TV Channel*, www.history.co.uk/articles/asgard-and-the-nine-worlds-of-norse-mythology. Accessed May 20, 2022.

Atkins, Harry. "10 of the Most Important Vikings." *History Hit*, 2018, www.historyhit.com/the-most-important-vikings/.

"Babies and Vikings." *An Outpouring of Thought*, dyannehs.tumblr.com/post/82616037578/babies-and-vikings. Accessed May 20, 2022.

Baptista, Fernando G., et al. "The Realm of the Vikings." *National Geographic*, https://www.nationalgeographic.com/specialprojects/interactive-assets/nggraphics/vikingsettlements-graphic/build-2017-03-27_16-28-31/#:~:text=Vikings%20used%20clinker%20design%E2%80%94overlapping,planks%20laid%20edge%20to%20edge. Accessed Aug. 28, 2022.

Barnett, David. "Norse Mythology Is Enjoying an Unlikely Renaissance in Popular Culture." *The Independent*, July 19, 2018, www.independent.co.uk/arts-entertainment/culture-norse-mythology-marvel-comics-film-christianity-neil-gaiman-american-gods-a8444321.html.

"Birth and Naming - Viking Culture." *Galnet Wiki*,
  galnet.fandom.com/wiki/Birth_and_naming_-
  _Viking_Culture.

Bolle, Kees W, and Jonathan Z Smith. "Myth." *Encyclopædia
  Britannica*, 2017, www.britannica.com/topic/myth.

Canadian Museum of History. "Egyptian Civilization - Myths -
  the Divine Family." *Www.historymuseum.ca*,
  www.historymuseum.ca/cmc/exhibitions/civil/egypt/egcr1
  oe.html.

Cavna, Michael. "STAN LEE: As 'Thor' Scores, Creator
  Considers Why the Superhero Film Endures." *The
  Washington Post*, May 11, 2011,
  https://www.washingtonpost.com/blogs/comic-
  riffs/post/stan-lee-as-thor-scores-creator-reveals-why-the-
  superhero-film-
  endures/2011/05/10/AF6rSpqG_blog.html.

Christensen, Christian. "15 Facts about Viking Women: Raiding,
  Marriage, Divorce, Rights, and More." *Scandinavia Facts*,
  scandinaviafacts.com/viking-women/.

---. "This Is How the Vikings Proposed and Got Married."
  Scandinavia Facts, scandinaviafacts.com/this-is-how-the-
  vikings-proposed-and-got-married/.

"Christianity Comes to Denmark." *National Museum of Denmark*, en.natmus.dk/historical-knowledge/denmark/prehistoric-period-until-1050-ad/the-viking-age/religion-magic-death-and-rituals/christianity-comes-to-denmark/#:~:text=The%20Christianization%20process&text=The%20Vikings%20regarded%20the%20new. Accessed May 21, 2022.

Christopoulou, Danai. "How Pop Culture Revived Norse Mythology." *Culture Trip*, theculturetrip.com/europe/norway/articles/how-pop-culture-revived-norse-mythology/.

Chrysoula. "Hades and Persephone Story." *Athens and Beyond*, May 10, 2021, athensandbeyond.com/hades-and-persephone-story/.

"The Clothes and Jewellery of the Vikings." *National Museum of Denmark*, 2019, en.natmus.dk/historical-knowledge/denmark/prehistoric-period-until-1050-ad/the-viking-age/the-people/clothes-and-jewellery/.

"Creation of the World in Norse Mythology." *Nordic Culture*, June 1, 2011, skjalden.com/creation-of-the-world-in-norse-mythology/.

Delgado, Daniel. "Legendary Characters from Norse Mythology." *MegaInteresting.com*, May 29, 2020,

www.megainteresting.com/history/gallery/legendary-
characters-from-norse-mythology-741590756208/1.

"*Der Ring Des Nibelungen.*" *Wikipedia*, 2022,
https://en.wikipedia.org/wiki/Der_Ring_des_Nibelungen.

"Difference between Myths and Folktales (with Table) – Ask
Any Difference." *Askanydifference.com*,
askanydifference.com/difference-between-myths-and-
folktales/.

Dimuro, Gina. "The Story of Shieldmaidens – the Viking
Warrior Women." *All That's Interesting*, Dec. 22, 2017,
allthatsinteresting.com/viking-shieldmaidens.

Felder, Grace. "11 Breathtaking Fantasy Books Inspired by
Norse Mythology." *The Portalist*, Apr. 19, 2022,
https://theportalist.com/norse-mythology-fantasy-books.

"Folklore | Academic Discipline | Britannica." *Encyclopædia
Britannica*, 2020, www.britannica.com/topic/folklore-
academic-discipline.

"Freya the Goddess of Love and Fertility - Norse Mythology."
Nordic Culture, Aug. 13, 2020,
skjalden.com/freya/#:~:text=Freya%20is%20the%20godd
ess%20of.

"Freyja." *World History Encyclopedia*,
www.worldhistory.org/Freyja/.

"Freyr." *World History Encyclopedia,*
www.worldhistory.org/Freyr/.

"Frigg – the Goddess of Marriage | the Swedish History
Museum." *Historiska.se*, historiska.se/norse-
mythology/frigg-
en/#:~:text=Frigg%20is%20the%20Queen%20of.

"Ginnungagap - the Yawning Void - Norse Mythology." *Nordic
Culture*, July 22, 2020, skjalden.com/ginnungagap/.

GreekBoston.com. "How Did Zeus Become King of the Gods?"
Greekboston.com, Mar. 24, 2016,
www.greekboston.com/culture/mythology/zeus-becomes-
king/.

Groeneveld, Emma. "Loki." *World History Encyclopedia*, Nov.
17, 2017, www.worldhistory.org/Loki/.

"Haggle." *Collins English Dictionary*,
https://www.collinsdictionary.com/us/dictionary/english/
haggle.

Hanson, Marilee. "Norse Mythology." *Englishhistory.net*, Oct.
27, 2016, englishhistory.net/vikings/norse-mythology/.

"Heimdall | Norse Mythology." *Encyclopædia Britannica*, 2019,
www.britannica.com/topic/Heimdall.

"Hel (Goddess) - Norse Mythology for Smart People." *Norse Mythology for Smart People*, 2012, norse-mythology.org/gods-and-creatures/giants/hel/.

"Hel Is NOT the Norse Goddess of Death - Norse Mythology." *Nordic Culture*, Aug. 27, 2020, skjalden.com/hel/.

History.com Editors. "Vikings." *HISTORY*, A&E Television Networks, Nov. 4, 2009, www.history.com/topics/exploration/vikings-history.

"How Norse Mythology Has Influenced Popular Culture» Scandipop.co.uk." *Scandipop.co.uk*, Sept. 28, 2020, scandipop.co.uk/norse-mythology-influenced-popular-culture/.

"How the Great Myths and Legends Were Created." *Writers Store*, writersstore.com/blogs/news/how-the-great-myths-and-legends-were-created.

"How Vikings Actually Looked (Complete Guide to Viking Traits)." *Nordicperspective.com*, nordicperspective.com/history/vikings/how-vikings-actually-looked-complete-guide.

https://www.facebook.com/learn.religions. "Learn the Basics behind the Norse Runes." *Learn Religions*, 2019, www.learnreligions.com/norse-runes-basic-overview-2562815.

https://www.facebook.com/norman.sheppard. "The Origins of the Norse Mythology | the Norse Gods." *The Norse Gods*, June 30, 2018, thenorsegods.com/the-origins-of-the-norse-mythology/.

"Hurstwic: Clothing in the Viking Age." *Hurstwic.org*, 2019, www.hurstwic.org/history/articles/daily_living/text/clothing.htm.

"Hurstwic: Viking Ships." *Hurstwic.org*, 2015, www.hurstwic.org/history/articles/manufacturing/text/norse_ships.htm.

"Japanese Folklore and Mythology." *New World Encyclopedia*, https://www.newworldencyclopedia.org/entry/japanese_folklore_and_mythology.

"Japanese Mythology: 6 Japanese Mythical Creatures." *TheCollector*, Dec. 28, 2021, www.thecollector.com/japanese-mythical-creatures-mythology/.

JOURNALIST, Irene Berg Petersen, and VIDENSKAB.DK. "What Vikings Really Looked Like." *Sciencenordic.com*, July 29, 2012, sciencenordic.com/archaeology-denmark-history/what-vikings-really-looked-like/1374457#:~:text=%E2%80%9CFrom%20picture%20sources%20we%20know.

Kumar, Abhay. "How Vikings & Norse Mythology Are Making Its Way into the Modern Entertainment." *Medium*, May 7, 2020, medium.com/nerdvolume/how-vikings-norse-mythology-are-making-its-way-into-the-modern-entertainment-f148c15c1d52.

Kuroski, John. "Meet Olga of Kyiv, the Viking Ruler Who Became Ukraine's "Patron Saint" of Vengeance." *All That's Interesting*, Apr. 15, 2022, allthatsinteresting.com/olga-of-kiev. Accessed 20 May 2022.

"Laugardagr." *Wiktionary*, 2022, https://en.wiktionary.org/wiki/laugardagr.

"Legend | Literature." *Encyclopædia Britannica*, 2019, www.britannica.com/art/legend-literature.

Loïc. "15 Famous Vikings Warriors You Need to Know About." *Norse and Viking Mythology [Best Blog] - Vkngjewelry*, Feb. 5, 2019, blog.vkngjewelry.com/en/famous-vikings/.

"Making a Viking Ship." *Regia Anglorum*, https://regia.org/research/ships/Ships1.htm. Accessed Aug. 28, 2022.

McIntosh, Matthew A. "Viking Artistic Development and Stylistic Influences on Later Scandinavian, Anglo-Saxon, and Western European Romanesque Art and Architecture." *Brewminate*, May 4, 2016, brewminate.com/viking-artistic-development-and-stylistic-influences-on-later-scandinavian-anglo-saxon-and-western-european-romanesque-art-and-architecture/.

Manual, Byline. "Viking History: Facts & Myths." *Live Science*, Aug. 29, 2018, www.livescience.com/32087-viking-history-facts-myths.html.

Mark, Joshua J. "Fenrir." *World History Encyclopedia*, Aug. 25, 2021, https://www.worldhistory.org/Fenrir/.

---. "Mythology." *World History Encyclopedia*, Oct. 31, 2018, www.worldhistory.org/mythology/.

---. "Sleipnir." *World History Encyclopedia*, Aug. 30, 2021, https://www.worldhistory.org/Sleipnir/.

Mason, Emma. "A Brief History of the Vikings." *History Extra*, Nov. 26, 2018, www.historyextra.com/period/viking/vikings-history-facts/.

McCoy, Daniel. "Death and the Afterlife - Norse Mythology for Smart People." *Norse Mythology for Smart People*, 2012, norse-mythology.org/concepts/death-and-the-afterlife/.

---. "Heimdall - Norse Mythology for Smart People." *Norse Mythology for Smart People*, https://norse-mythology.org/gods-and-creatures/the-aesir-gods-and-goddesses/heimdall/.

---. "Loki - Norse Mythology for Smart People." *Norse Mythology for Smart People*, 2009, norse-mythology.org/gods-and-creatures/the-aesir-gods-and-goddesses/loki/.

---. "Odin - Norse Mythology for Smart People." *Norse Mythology for Smart People*, 2012, norse-mythology.org/gods-and-creatures/the-aesir-gods-and-goddesses/odin/.

---. "The Aesir-Vanir War." *Norse Mythology for Smart People*, norse-mythology.org/tales/the-aesir-vanir-war/.

---. "The Creation of the Cosmos - Norse Mythology for Smart People." *Norse Mythology for Smart People*, 2012, norse-mythology.org/tales/norse-creation-myth/.

McKay, Andrew. "Creatures in Norse Mythology." *Life in Norway*, July 19, 2018, www.lifeinnorway.net/creatures-in-norse-mythology/.

"Medieval Scandinavian Architecture." *Wikipedia*, Nov. 22, 2019, en.wikipedia.org/wiki/Medieval_Scandinavian_architecture.

Milner, Richard. "What Life Was like for Viking Women." *Grunge.com*, 5 July 2020, www.grunge.com/223423/what-life-was-like-for-viking-women/. Accessed May 20, 2022.

Morgan, Thad. "How Did the Vikings Honor Their Dead?" *HISTORY*, www.history.com/news/how-did-the-vikings-honor-their-dead#:~:text=Cremation%20.

National Museum of Denmark. "Women - National Museum of Denmark." *National Museum of Denmark*, 2019, en.natmus.dk/historical-knowledge/denmark/prehistoric-period-until-1050-ad/the-viking-age/the-people/women/.

"Nine Realms of Norse Cosmology." *World History Encyclopedia*, www.worldhistory.org/article/1305/nine-realms-of-norse-cosmology/.

Nix, Elizabeth. "6 Viking Leaders You Should Know." *HISTORY*, Sept. 4, 2018, www.history.com/news/6-viking-leaders-you-should-know.

"Njord." *Mythopedia*, mythopedia.com/topics/njord.

"Njord - Norse Mythology for Smart People." *Norse Mythology for Smart People*, 2012, norse-mythology.org/gods-and-creatures/the-vanir-gods-and-goddesses/njord/.

"Norns Are the Personifications of the Past, the Present, and the Future." *Nordic Culture*, Sept. 4, 2020, https://skjalden.com/norns/.

"Norse Ghosts & Funerary Rites." *World History Encyclopedia*, www.worldhistory.org/article/1291/norse-ghosts--funerary-rites/.

"Norse Mythology | Encyclopedia.com."
Www.encyclopedia.com,
www.encyclopedia.com/humanities/news-wires-white-
papers-and-books/norse-mythology.

"Odin's Discovery of the Runes." *Norse Mythology for Smart
People*, norse-mythology.org/tales/odins-discovery-of-the-
runes/.

Pruitt, Sarah. "What Was Life like for Women in the Viking
Age?" *HISTORY*, Mar. 5, 2019,
www.history.com/news/what-was-life-like-for-women-in-
the-viking-age.

"Ragnarök." *World History Encyclopedia*,
www.worldhistory.org/Ragnarok/.

Rai, Mridu. "7 Fascinating Indian Folk Tales." *Culture Trip*,
Mar. 27, 2018, theculturetrip.com/asia/india/articles/7-
fascinating-indian-folk-tales/.

Rodgers, David Gray. "The Viking Shield - A Historic Look."
Sons of Vikings, Apr. 25, 2018,
https://sonsofvikings.com/blogs/history/the-viking-
shield-a-historic-look.

"Rollo of Normandy." *World History Encyclopedia*,
www.worldhistory.org/Rollo_of_Normandy/.

Rouă, Victor. "Architecture in the Viking Age: Urban Planning, Emporia, and Strongholds." *The Dockyards*, Oct. 22, 2016, www.thedockyards.com/architecture-viking-age-urban-planning-emporia-strongholds/.

Royal Museums Greenwich. "Viking Ships." *Www.rmg.co.uk*, 2021, www.rmg.co.uk/stories/topics/viking-ships.

"Runes." *World History Encyclopedia*, www.worldhistory.org/runes/.

S, Jessica. "Viking Clothing History : What Did the Vikings Wear?" *Norse and Viking Mythology [Best Blog] - Vkngjewelry*, Mar. 4, 2019, blog.vkngjewelry.com/en/viking-clothing-history/.

---. "What Did Vikings Really Look Like?" *Norse and Viking Mythology [Best Blog] - Vkngjewelry*, May 6, 2019, blog.vkngjewelry.com/en/what-did-vikings-really-look-like/.

"Skaldic Poetry." *Britannica*, Nov. 8, 2015, https://www.britannica.com/art/skaldic-poetry.

"Social Classes in Viking Society." *Nordic Culture*, Aug. 17, 2018, skjalden.com/viking-social-classes/.

"Sol and Mani - Norse Mythology for Smart People." *Norse Mythology for Smart People*, 2014, norse-mythology.org/sol-mani/.

Sons of Vikings. "Viking Lore: A Quick Intro to Norse Eddas and Sagas." https://sonsofvikings.com/blogs/history/viking-lore-a-quick-intro-to-norse-eddas-and-sagas.

Sturluson, Snorri. (1916). *The Prose Edda: Gylfaginning* (A.G. Brodeur, Trans.). https://www.sacred-texts.com/neu/pre/pre04.htm (Original work published ca. 1200 A.D.).

The Editors of Encyclopedia Britannica. "Ragnarök | Scandinavian Mythology." *Encyclopædia Britannica*, 2019, www.britannica.com/event/Ragnarok.

The Editors of Encyclopedia Britannica. "Viking | History, Exploration, Facts, & Maps." *Encyclopædia Britannica*, Aug. 24, 2018, www.britannica.com/topic/Viking-people.

"The Hidden Meanings behind Viking Runes." *History Hit*, www.historyhit.com/the-hidden-meanings-behind-viking-runes/. Accessed May 20, 2022.

"The Myth of Hades and Persephone." *Greek Myths & Greek Mythology*, Nov. 10, 2010, www.greekmyths-greekmythology.com/myth-of-hades-and-persephone/#:~:text=Hades%20fell%20in%20love%20with.

"The Nine Realms in Norse Mythology." *Nordic Culture*, June 1, 2011, skjalden.com/nine-realms-in-norse-mythology/.

"The Poetic Edda: Grímnismál." *Www.germanicmythology.com*, www.germanicmythology.com/PoeticEdda/GRM40.html. Accessed May 20, 2022.

"The Punishment of Loki." *BaviPower*, bavipower.com/blogs/bavipower-viking-blog/the-punishment-of-loki.

"The Viking Social Structure - Norse Mythology for Smart People." *Norse Mythology for Smart People*, 2017, norse-mythology.org/viking-social-structure/.

"Thor | Germanic Deity." *Encyclopedia Britannica*, www.britannica.com/topic/Thor-Germanic-deity.

"Thor's Goats." *Nordic Culture*, Sept. 5, 2020, https://skjalden.com/thors-goats/.

"Tyr | Germanic Deity." *Encyclopedia Britannica*, www.britannica.com/topic/Tyr.

"Vali." *Norse Mythology for Smart People*, norse-mythology.org/vali/.

"Vanir - New World Encyclopedia." *Www.newworldencyclopedia.org*, www.newworldencyclopedia.org/entry/Vanir.

"Vidar." *Norse Mythology for Smart People*, norse-mythology.org/vidar/#:~:text=Vidar%20(pronounced%20%E2%80%9CVIH%2Ddar. Accessed May 20, 2022.

"Viking Art - the History of Norse and Viking Artwork." *Artincontext.org*, June 2, 2021, artincontext.org/viking-art/.

"Viking Funerals: Prayers, Pyre & Traditions | Cake Blog." *Www.joincake.com*, www.joincake.com/blog/viking-funeral/.

"Viking Ships and Shipbuilding." *Danishnet.com*, Aug. 24, 2016, www.danishnet.com/vikings/viking-ships-and-shipbuilding/.

"Vikings and Religion." *Sons of Vikings*, Mar. 26, 2019, sonsofvikings.com/blogs/history/the-vikings-and-christianity.

"Vikings, Paganism and the Gods." *Medieval Chronicles*, www.medievalchronicles.com/medieval-history/medieval-history-periods/vikings/vikings-paganism-and-the-gods/.

"Vikings: From Pagans to Christians - History." *History*, May 29, 2018, www.historyonthenet.com/vikings-from-pagans-to-christians.

VikingsBrand. "The Death and the Afterlife in Norse Mythology." *VikingsBrand*, www.vikingsbrand.co/blogs/norse-news/the-death-and-the-afterlife-in-norse-mythology.

Wallace, Birgitta. "Vinland | Historical Area, North America." *Britannica*, https://www.britannica.com/place/Vinland. Accessed Sept. 4, 2022.

"What Do We Know about Viking Funerals?" *HistoryExtra*, www.historyextra.com/period/viking/viking-funerals-burning-ships-grave-goods-oseberg-ship/.

"What's the Difference between a Myth, a Legend, a Folktale, and a Fairytale?" *Irish Myths*, Feb. 20, 2021, irishmyths.com/2021/02/20/differences-between-myths-legends-folktales-fairytales/. Accessed 20 May 2022.

"Where Did They Come From?" *JORVIK Viking Centre*, www.jorvikvikingcentre.co.uk/the-vikings/where-did-they-come-from/.

"Why Did the English People Stop Eating Horses in the Middle Ages?" *Medievalists.net*, https://www.medievalists.net/2013/02/why-did-the-english-people-stop-eating-horses-in-the-middle-ages/. Accessed Aug. 30, 2022.

"Why Do We Know So Little About Viking Helmets?" *History with Hilbert*, May 20, 2020, https://www.youtube.com/watch?v=XR91MAu6zKU

Wikipedia Contributors. "Old Norse Religion." *Wikipedia, Wikimedia Foundation*, Nov. 12, 2019, en.wikipedia.org/wiki/Old_Norse_religion.

---. "Prose Edda." Wikipedia, Wikimedia Foundation, Mar. 19, 2019, en.wikipedia.org/wiki/Prose_Edda.

---. "Viking Expansion." *Wikipedia*, Wikimedia Foundation, Jan. 28, 2019, en.wikipedia.org/wiki/Viking_expansion.

Williams, Gareth. "BBC - History - Ancient History in Depth: Viking Religion." *Bbc.co.uk*, 2011, www.bbc.co.uk/history/ancient/vikings/religion_01.shtml.

"Women in the Viking Age." *World History Encyclopedia*, www.worldhistory.org/article/1251/women-in-the-viking-age/.

"Yggdrasil and the 9 Norse Worlds." *HeritageDaily - Archaeology News*, Aug. 2, 2018, www.heritagedaily.com/2018/08/yggdrasil-and-the-9-norse-worlds/121244.

"Ymir." *Norse Mythology for Smart People*, norse-mythology.org/gods-and-creatures/giants/ymir/.